# Cultural Heritage Collaborators

## A Manual for Community Documentation

Melissa Mannon

ArchivesInfo Press • New Hampshire

Library of Congress Cataloging-in-Publication Data
Mannon, Melissa
Cultural Heritage Collaborators: A Manual for Community Documentation / Melissa Mannon.
p. cm.

Includes bibliographical references and index.

ISBN-13: 978-0-982-72760-7

1. Archives—Administration. 2. Public history—United States.

Cover photo by Melissa Mannon

www.archivesinfo.com

TO KEVIN, my number one collaborator

# Contents

# Acknowledgments

Thank you to the archives caretakers — archivists, librarians, museum professionals, volunteers, and town clerks — who so freely shared their knowledge and experiences to help provide the model samples used in this book. I would like to thank: representatives from the St. Johnsbury Collaborative — Patricia Swartz, Ann Lawless, Shara McCaffery, Charlie Browne, and Selene Colburn; Sarah Dunlap and Janie Walsh of the Gloucester Collaborative; Samantha Grantham and Lindsay Diehl of the Wenham Museum; Richard Trask of the Danvers Archives; Jim Martin of the Wildwood Historical Society; Montana State Archivist Jodie Foley and Molly Kruckenberg of the Montana Historical Society; Jane Pieplow from the Churchill County Museum and Archives; Pamela Cooley from the New York State Archives; John Ansley from Marist College; staff from Hershey Community Archives and The Hershey Story — Tammy Hamilton, Amy Bischof, and Valerie Seiber; Kara Fossey from Groton Historical Society Museum; and Greg Jordan of Lynn County Historical Society. I give special thanks to Nancy Schrock, whose professionalism and work in Winchester have provided me with inspiration for many years.

Thank you also to my early mentors: Vicki Wright of the Kalamazoo Institute of Arts and formerly from the University of New Hampshire; Nancy Noble of the Maine Historical Society and formerly from the Portsmouth Public Library; Maureen Melton of the Museum of Fine Arts; and Meghan Sniffon-Marinoff of the Harvard University

Archives, formerly from Simmons College. These wonderful women were the first to set me down the archives path and made me think about collections on a broad scale. Thank you also to Tom Jewell and Kate Tranquada, the former and current directors of the Waltham Public Library, who gave me the freedom early in my career to explore collaborative endeavors and to think about the possibilities of cross-professional collaboration.

Thank you to all of my consulting clients who have allowed me to help guide them in their archives management and collaborative endeavors. Without them, the ideas found in this book would never have found form in my personal theory or practice. I want to specifically thank Sarah Brophy, formerly of the Carlisle Historical Society and current principal of bMuse, who served on a regional panel with me to discuss some of the ideas presented in this book and has spent much time over the years helping me mold ideas about our work. She continually offers me professional support and collegial friendship. I also want to specifically thank William Whiting of Topsfield, who also served on the panel with me and whose shining work within his community of Topsfield, Massachusetts, though not represented in this book, should serve as a model for all.

Thank you to the reference librarians of the Bedford Public Library for their hard work locating the resources I needed. Thank you also to my editor Jennifer Gidman Zumpano, whose skills helped make a clean manuscript and whose support helped guide me to the finish. I also want to recognize Michelle Sampson of the Wadleigh Memorial Library and Erica Holthausen of Joppa Communications for their support.

Finally, I am grateful to my husband Kevin and daughter Lorelei for their infinite patience, encouragement, and love.

# Introduction

A session I chaired at a regional museum conference discussed promoting local cultural heritage organizations through collaborative archives ventures. The panel focused our presentation on historical societies and small museums, which usually serve as the linchpins for local history projects. The speakers included representatives from various-sized communities in Massachusetts that conducted archival surveys and used consulting services to guide them in collaborative endeavors. Our session aimed to show how underutilized, under-cared-for, and underfunded historical resources could be revitalized and could become a showpiece for one's institution and town. We explored how to begin a project to gain control of collections. We emphasized that archives collaboration could help the overall mission of an institution.

One audience member particularly struck me. At the end of the session, she stood up and said that the ideas we discussed are ones she had been contemplating and has slowly started bandying to organizations in her town. However, she had been hesitant to speak to local institutions, afraid that her ideas were too unusual and that she was stepping on toes. Our session helped the audience realize that movement toward community collaboration was a forward-thinking concept. Working together, institutions that handle the cultural resources of a community could better raise awareness of local history, the management needs of local historical materials, and the ways such resources can boost a town or city.

"Collaboration" is becoming the new buzzword in the nonprofit community. In an effort to reinvent ourselves during changing times, cultural heritage institutions such as archives, libraries, and museums are forging new partnerships. In a time when so much information is right at our fingertips, our users expect us to be "plugged in." Gone are the days when cultural institutions could operate in a vacuum with their eyes on their own bottom line and mission statement. We now must meld into the world around us, creating new networks that provide more efficient pathways to information. The cultural resources we possess can become a backbone for knowledge and community identities, creating an accurate documentary record that reflects our towns, its citizens, and the world in which we live.

It is unusual and difficult for institutions to reprioritize, putting the goals of the many ahead of the one. Working with others is often no easy task. But cultural heritage institutions must recognize that our success (and, indeed, our very existence) depends on how our presence is perceived by our communities. While budgets are slashed, we have the opportunity to position ourselves as vital to society. The alternative is to fade away with our limited funds and limited audiences.

Partnerships between the historical societies my fellow speakers represented, local libraries, town governments, educational institutions, associations, and local businesses have allowed them to gain a more visible community presence. Viewing their examples, audience members saw tangible evidence that organizations can come together with a common goal of sustaining a sense of community through the promotion of cultural heritage resources. By connecting cultural organizations to the heart of a community's pulse and character, we can create a stronger awareness of our vitality and how we can benefit diverse members of society. If we love history, we know that the historical materials that cultural heritage repositories maintain are important for preserving our past, defining our identity, and highlighting the individual's purpose as a member of a larger whole. It is our challenge as keepers of collections to convince others of the worthiness of our mission.

There is a long-established, natural bond between cultural heritage institutions of all sorts. In the world of professionally run cultural heritage institutions, museums, libraries, and archives preserve and pass on culture, serve as civic centers, assist economic development, work as recreational centers, and play an important lifelong educational role for their patrons. All possess resources that reflect culture and help us evaluate society. For decades, these institutions have operated in distinctly separate spheres with diversely trained and degreed professionals who use separate theories for operation. Alternately, volunteer-based organizations tend to meld the care of artifacts, publications, and archives. While librarians, archivists, and museum personnel work to bring their professions closer so that they may collaborate, they must also recognize the partnerships they are required to forge with their nonprofessional colleagues to attain success. Historically, cultural heritage institutions have always had shared missions. It is time for us to reexplore them and make them part of our everyday thinking. [1] We must acknowledge our differences and explore parallels, maintaining distinct identities and practices while leaning on similarities to forge collaborative partnerships among all ranks of cultural heritage workers.

---

1. Carmine J. Bell, in her article "Public Education and Community Development: The Shared Mission of Libraries and Cultural Heritage Institution" (available online), outlines a history of the shared goals of cultural institutions. When museums and libraries were first founded in the United States, they often were within the same institution with more blurred lines of authority and procedures than we see today.

This book focuses on the role of archival resources in our missions. It discusses the value of archives for creating an accurate documentary record and for supporting our other collections. The fields of librarianship, museology, and archives management follow distinct practices today, yet they are all similar in that those who work in these fields are the handlers of many of our civilization's most culturally significant materials. These include resources that enhance identity and intellectual development. I have worked in all three fields in various stages of my education and career. I propose that it is records that have the greatest capacity for pulling local organizations together as a cultural collaborative. The creation and maintenance of records is threaded through everything that we do as a society. Everyone makes records, and everyone needs to maintain them, file them, or dispose of them. Records exist in a multitude of formats in every institution and every residence in the United States.

The audience for this book includes anyone handling historical records, in any setting, at any level of employ. Professionals familiar with managing archives will benefit from its review of theory, overarching perspective, and collaborative discussion. It will help them place their work as part of a bigger picture and offer ways to effectively collaborate and relate to people outside of their professional circle. Nonprofessionals and professionals in related fields will further benefit from the book's introduction to archival methods of collection management and collection development, and from a brief overview of archives terminology. Gathering a little basic knowledge based on professional standards will help non-archivists effectively administer the archival material in their care. This book outlines how to begin caring for collections in any setting so that those new to these concepts will come away with a sense of professionalism.

In the past few years, the subject of collaboration between cultural heritage institutions has gained notoriety in professional literature. Yet, due to a shared history dating to the nineteenth century, when small museums were often housed in local libraries, and more recently due to the mandate of the Institute of Museum and Library Services and the 1996 Museum and Library Services Act, most studies have focused on the links between libraries and museums. Archives are mentioned as an aside or not at all. It is my intention to change the focus a bit. The artifacts and books handled by cultural institutions will benefit by increased attention on archives. As we focus our record collecting, so, too, are we better able to focus all of our collecting strategies. Furthermore, archives collection development is recommended as a first step toward redistributing our energies to collaborative collection development, which can then be followed by other cooperative activities.

Within the masses of records we generate are those that have special import. Unfortunately, we often lose these among the mounds of papers that we accumulate regularly. When we refer to archives, we mean the noteworthy, unique, culturally reflective, recorded resources that require special care to ensure the continuance of society and knowledge. Archival records are made every day, yet their creators do not always recognize their value. Archives help form our community memories and shape our beliefs about history and the future. We need to identify them as distinct among the piles of documents that civilized societies create. This book discusses how to distinguish them and how to help others recognize them, too.

With a little planning, archives and records management can increase understanding about the need for maintaining our cultural resources and recognizing the importance of the things that we create — of our material culture — in general. As repositories that collect records, we must raise awareness about archives, work to preserve them, and ensure that we are creating well-balanced collections of diverse materials offering multiple points of view. The best way to do this is for all organizations collecting local history materials to collaborate and create solid collection development policies based on collaborative work. This book emphasizes the need to form a solid foundation of collecting practices before pursuing other projects. These practices can form the base of operations to help make a cultural repository "successful."

Though there are archivists, librarians, curators, historians, clerks, secretaries, volunteers, and private collectors who purposefully care for archival resources, many do not formalize their collecting plans or adequately review their collecting goals. Both professional archivists and "amateur" record keepers collect to document the history of their town or a chosen theme. Their goal is to create a "documentary record" of these subjects. Those without collecting policies do not adequately pay attention to documentation gaps or redundancy in collecting practices. Generally, collectors gather and preserve materials in areas that interest them or in areas where they perceive a dearth of collecting activity.

Efforts to collect materials frequently compete with the collecting activities of neighbors or other organizations to which an organization has some sort of intellectual connection. In an attempt to document history, record keepers spread themselves thin while trying to gather historical records relating to broad topics. The quantity of records available in such a broad area is generally so vast that it is impossible for anyone to gather them alone. There are certainly enough materials to go around so that every repository that wishes to do so can find an appropriate collecting niche. Broad gaps in documentation often occur because of the competitive aspect of collecting that many institutions adopt, trying to get the most "valuable" materials related to the most prominent citizens in a community. Furthermore, many collect insignificant manuscripts lacking the depth of information that is most beneficial to researchers and society, just to keep a document that was written by someone noteworthy or that pertains to a subject they perceive as important. The collections of miscellaneous materials that are gathered come complete with large gaps in the information they are trying to reveal, while still overlapping with the readily available information kept by one's neighbors.

Within this book are samples of a variety of repositories collecting and maintaining archives. These models serve to show how a community can deal with its documentation in a number of ways. It is not necessary to have a formal, centralized archives repository. Though I think having one is beneficial, many communities are working to adequately maintain their records through the historical societies, libraries, town halls, and other repositories that already exist within their communities. Dedicated volunteers, sympathetic government leaders, and knowledgeable professionals in non-archives fields have been able to start grassroots programs that try to make do with what they have or work hard to raise awareness and develop more professionally run archives-management programs. The intention of this book is to show that it doesn't matter what kind of archives program you have now: It is possible to propel attempts to organize projects through collaboration. It is possible to begin a strong commitment to archives management with a focus on collection development and planning, with even a minimal budget. It is possible to make things better, even when we cannot make things perfect.

There is a dire need to rethink our collecting practices to ensure that we are properly documenting multiple historical perspectives related to the broad range of human activities and knowledge. This book discusses the need to better plan what archival material we will collect through archival appraisal, how to focus our own collections, and how to collaborate with others to most effectively preserve our history and heritage. It shows why collaboration and collection development must operate in tandem to be most successful.

Like other books in the field, *Cultural Heritage Collaborators: A Manual for Community Documentation* discusses the steps for writing collection development policies and for making collecting decisions. It discusses using collection development as a foundation for all activities relating to archives in any cultural organization. It discusses how to do the planning necessary before a policy is actually written. Unlike other books, it presents these steps with a collaborative approach. It describes differing ideology and methods among diverse cultural heritage professionals with an eye toward merging philosophies and overcoming hurdles related to varying views and terminology. It promotes active relationships with partner institutions for collecting and collaborative outreach strategies to attract potential donors and collection users. The book encourages institutions to incorporate a community documentation strategy. Such a strategy allows local repositories to find a collecting niche in their community, in a noncompetitive fashion, to actively seek records related to their mission, and to work with other repositories to create a collecting network that seeks to be all-inclusive, focused, and accessible.

Beyond the scope of this book is a detailed discussion of the varying collaborative activities an institution can pursue beyond collection development. However, this book suggests collection development as a means to begin successful collaboration without an atmosphere of competition for resources, opening the doors for collaborative efforts in additional areas. It is often difficult for historical organizations to gain the support they need to adequately perform preservation, outreach, and digitization. Two or more organizations working to raise awareness about cultural resources will increase their exposure and hence find more individuals willing to help fund, volunteer, and sustain them. If Archives, museums, libraries, town governments, businesses, and local associations work together to create optimal collecting programs, it will lead to more successful activities in all areas of historical preservation and information dissemination.

For an archives program to flourish and to perform collection development efficiently, it must have a strong sense of self. An archivist must be able to define the role her archives play in the community. You must be prepared to show outsiders that the institution is organized and is a vital entity with an important function. A vital step toward developing an image is to perform an internal survey of records that allows you to gain a better understanding of the scope of holdings, their strengths, and their weaknesses. This book ends with how to conduct a constructive survey project to further collection development and collaborative goals.

Earlier in this introduction, I put forth the notion that proper beginning practices are necessary for any cultural organization to be "successful." I have some model examples to share, but I also have stories of organizations that gather steam and fade. I have seen others muddle along with limited resources or attention. Some cultural institutions achieve a modicum of success with interesting programs and collections but no grand plans for the future. I want every cultural institution to see "success" as the following:

1. A cultural institution is successful when it has a focused collection of interesting materials and a plan for further

collecting that makes its resources more reflective of the community with which it is involved.
2. A cultural institution is successful when it provides ready access to its cultural materials through "finding aids" or other access tools that are easily shared with outsiders.
3. A cultural institution is successful when it has the resources it needs (including personnel and monetary support) to accomplish everyday tasks and to move the institution forward following established goals and a long-range plan.
4. A cultural institution is successful when it is viewed by the majority of residents in its locale or its alternative target audience as a vital part of the community, invoking a sense of community spirit and standing as a place that reflects a sense of identity.

Our documentary heritage is in danger. Materials are lost every day due to neglect and mishandling within and outside of cultural heritage institutions. This book encourages individuals to take a proactive approach to the management of cultural resources. Begin thinking about the nature, value, and condition of collections. Then take the first step toward caring for them by teaming with others to determine the needs of a community and the collections at hand. Aim to identify those documents needed to create a complete story about our society. No matter what the current condition of your collections, a thoughtful review of your situation and a collaborative planned approach will enable you to achieve success.

The ultimate goal of this book is to show how through planning, management basics, and tying oneself to a community through collaborative operations, you can make your institution stronger and its mission more manageable. By rethinking the role a repository plays in archives management, you can come to be regarded as an integral presence within the community. Collaboration will ensure the security of our cultural heritage, its documentation, and the nonprofit cultural institution.

**Hallmarks of a Successful Cultural Institution**

- Maintains Collection **Focus**
  - Uses a mission statement to guide the institution
  - Has established a collecting niche
  - Actively uses and promotes a collections policy that provides guidance for the future growth of collections
- Provides **Access**
  - Creates finding aids and other access tools and makes them available to the public
  - Remains open for a regular, set number of hours each week or makes it easy to arrange appointments to accommodate researchers
- Has **Support**
  - Employs staff or has a stable volunteer program to provide consistency and expert knowledge for maintaining collections
  - Has backing of an administrative body that provides consistent funding for overhead, programs, and other institutional needs
- Has **Status**
  - Invokes community spirit and reflects a sense of identity
  - Is recognized and touted as a vital community entity by the public

# 1. Who, What, & Why of Collecting Historical Records

A variety of institutions and individuals share the burden of safekeeping our historical records and our documented history. It is important to define exactly who they are, what they are collecting, and why to understand the significance of our own collecting mission. Without a deep comprehension of our work as assemblers of archival materials, we cannot properly explain to others the value of what we do. Our efforts to save our history must not be reduced to collecting for the sake of collecting itself — they must be explained in the cultural context of preserving society's knowledge and community identity.

Archivists, librarians, curators, town clerks, association secretaries, small-business and nonprofit administrators, and private individuals all collect significant enriching documents that are part of the material culture that helps provide this sense of "connectedness." "Material Culture is a vital element in the constitution and dynamics of all societies because of two essential factors: it is the product of the interaction of people and their materials worlds; and it is one of the principal means by which culture is stored and transmitted."[2] Some collect cultural items as professionals in traditional archival establishments, including university Archives and special collections, government Archives, business Archives, or

2. F. Leibrick cited in Christina Kreps, *Liberating Culture: Cross-Cultural Perspectives on Museums, Curations and Heritage Preservation*. (London: Routledge, 2003), 49.

standalone Special Collections (such as those found in large historical societies). Professional archivists may receive training in one of a variety of fields, including most notably the fields of history or library science.[3] Alternately, some who care for documents with historical significance may have no training at all, collecting as volunteers or getting on-the-job training within their communities, caring for historical records in small historical societies and local museums. A third group, and one that is often forgotten or discounted, is history enthusiasts or fans of material culture who seek cultural items that have particular meaning to them as individuals, gathering things that have sentimental, aesthetic, or monetary value.[4] Even families without a strict interest in "collecting" are part of the collecting community, gathering and preserving their own records and personal family papers that have been passed from generation to generation.

Institutions often collect only the historical documents that they create, recording the history of their organization and ensuring vital documents are saved to ensure a foundation for the successful continuance of the group. Most such organizations collect administrative

---

3. A 1998 study by the Council of State Historical Records Coordinators classified the various types of repositories collecting records in three groups, and it is these three groups that have the prime responsibility for safeguarding our cultural resources and ensuring their comprehensiveness. The first group of record collectors is the professional core, including state and national Archives, large historical societies, university Archives, and private repositories. The second group is the "multifunctional" group encompassing repositories that collect archives in addition to their many other professional functions and may or may not see archives management as a prime responsibility. This group includes public libraries, museums, small corporations, schools, businesses, churches, and fraternal organizations. The third group consists of community-based organizations such as small historical societies. See Victoria Irons Walch, comp. *Where History Begins: A Report on Historical Records Repositories in the United States* (Council of State Historical Records Coordinators, May 1998), 37.
4. Sentimental, aesthetic, or monetary value is called "intrinsic value" in the archives field. Usually, professional collectors (archivists, curators, and librarians) determine the cultural significance of collections using professional theories and standards that evaluate the overall quality of information in addition to the materials' intrinsic value, whereas individual collectors rely primarily on the intrinsic.

documents that promote their institutions and/or the non-archival culturally important materials in their possession. Together with their archivist colleagues, caretakers of record collections outside traditional archival establishments work toward preserving the documents that retain their history. These "default archivists," who in some literature are called "accidental archivists" and include non-archivist professionals and volunteers in local multifunctional institutions that collect archives, are often the prime protectors of community and local history.[5] What their collections "offer is a sense of identity, an affirmation of individuality, and evidence of continuity" that is necessary for the continued functioning of an organization and society, and for the preservation of community.[6] The records with long-term value in any institution have the capacity to educate, providing evidence of human activity and offering insight into societal norms. For cultural heritage collaboratives to achieve success, they must recognize communal goals and the mutual benefits of involving all holders of valuable records in discussions about protecting documents and building collections, whatever the caretaker's background or institution's circumstances.

Cultural heritage resources (also known as material culture) include documents, artifacts, publications, and historic buildings that embody cultural knowledge and shed light on the functions and functioning of society. Archives are one form of culturally significant resources. They are original, unique documents created by the participants of an event or activity. They include manuscripts (one-of-a-kind written records), ledgers, diaries, photographs, original

---

5. The term "archivist" in this book is used loosely to describe any individual, professional or otherwise, who is charged with caring for historical documents.
6. Robert Archibald, *A Place to Remember: Using History to Build Community* (California: AltaMira Press, 1999), 177.

recordings including audio and visual formats (e.g., DVDs, recorded tapes, records), and digital material (e-mail, archived Web sites, CD-ROMs, etc.). Archives are not published materials, are not necessarily old, and are not always produced by well-known people. One may house archives in dedicated facilities that care for paper-based records only. Oftentimes, one may find these materials housed in mixed facilities that care for a variety of cultural resources.

**Definition of Archives**

The term "archives" is used in three different ways among those who collect historical materials.

First, it refers to records in any form that possess informational or some other long-term value and should therefore be permanently retained. Archivists most officially use this term for materials relating to the history of an institution that are kept permanently because of their evidential or informational value. The term is also used as an overarching concept to incorporate the idea of any documents with long-term value, but technically noninstitutional records are called personal papers. In this book, "archives" (with a lowercase "a") is used when talking about any documents and records.

Secondly, the term refers to the location at which archival materials are maintained. Thirdly, it refers to the organizational body that cares for archival materials – administration, staff, and guiding policies. In this book, "Archives" (with a capital "A") is used when discussing the place or organization that retains archival materials.

ability to bridge passing generations, and bring continuity and a sense of cultural connectedness. Thus material culture can play a critical role in the transmission of culture. Objects function in this way as a medium of communication."[7] They provide historical data about people, places, property, and events. They provide legal and financial data important to the administration and continuance of an institution. They assist with marketing, outreach, education, and research. Without archives, our political systems and business organizations would not retain their authority. Our progress would be inhibited due to lack of knowledge about past successes and failures. Without archives, a documentary record that relates the human story would be less accessible, focusing on interpretation of other culturally significant resources without accompanying contemporary written documentation.

Documents sustain the foundation of free and open governments. "Preservation of, public access to, and free and open debate over the content and interpretation of the past are essential to the health of American constitutional democracy. Enlightened discourse over critical issues, public policy, and the very nature of our democracy, requires continuous reference to the historical context."[8] Without the archives that document citizens' rights and define government's responsibilities, society cannot run efficiently, fairly, or responsibly.

One of the fundamental reasons for retaining information about our past is the need to preserve our heritage. Our sense of identity would be lacking without archives, for they help us to understand the past, giving rise to a shared sense of history that boosts a sense of

---

7. Kreps, *Liberating Culture*, 48.
8. American Association for State and Local History. *Support of State and Local Historical Agencies in America: A Statement of Concern* (July 2003).

community. "Civic, neighborhood, and familial life all depend on shared places that are repositories of common memories and shared experiences."[9] Archives represent — and even embody — those common memories that help define a community, including its sense of place, its people, and the events that formed it. With the passage of time, a place may become unrecognizable to those who experienced it in a particular moment. We must rely on individuals' recollections, or the artifacts and documents recording them, to gain an understanding and empathy for those who came before us. Archives help connect the memories between generations. These documents provide the tangible evidence of remembrances and impart a sense of what is past and how it brought us to where we are today. Archives can embolden us with our ancestors' wisdom to better understand the continuity of society.

The repositories that collect archives are important for the information they hold within their walls, but the institutions themselves also embody a unique identity because of this role. The civic institutions and privately endowed entities that exist to support our society's cultural and informational needs stand as testament to our civilization. Libraries, Archives, museums, and historical societies care for our cultural treasures, facilitate access to knowledge, and represent the ideals of American society. They show a culture with a special history worth preserving, helping to define our identities as Americans.

The small American archives repositories that collect local resources often seem valuable only to those concerned with a specific geographic region. But we must remember that the stories of individual communities have import beyond their immediate locale. Together, the documentary records of American communities tell the

---

9. Archibald, 17.

story of the nation and its people. Within these archives are stories of the most notable individuals in any given town who also may have participated on a regional or national stage, as well as lesser-known individuals. The local records related to their activities possess an immediacy that we usually cannot find elsewhere. Some of the events in which the individuals participated may have had a major impact on our development as a nation, and the records would reflect this. Other records may show the more mundane aspects of American lives.

One valuable lesson of collection development over the past thirty years has been that the archivist must ensure that all views of society are represented and that no one is left out of the historical collections that speak for our collective memory. It is the archivists' challenge to examine the scope of the collections in their care and to evaluate how well they reflect a culture as a whole from the details that seem obvious to the more outstanding. Collecting locally enables a more detailed look at this culture than that which could ever be done on a broader scale.

According to archival theorist Richard Cox, "The establishment of repositories for historical manuscripts and archives were often the direct activities of local historians who needed places to maintain the sources they were using."[10] Such collections developed primarily from the personal papers of individuals are called "special collections." Many such records are found in local historical societies that are collecting sources related to a particular town, another geographical locale, or a subject-related entity. Individuals who are aware of the historical and research value of their materials may look to donate their personal papers to such an archival repository for

---

10. Richard Cox, *Documenting Localities: A Practical Model for American Archivists and Manuscript Curators.* (Chicago: Society of American Archivists, 1996), 19.

safekeeping. Special collections also may include institutional papers of corporations and associations that do not wish to maintain their own archives. Or, such institutional records in Special collections may be from defunct organizations, their documents preserved to remember their place in society.

Unlike Special collections that gather materials from many different sources, institutional Archives focus on the materials created by one organization. Many institutions manage their own archives on-site. They may choose to manage their own records for legal, administrative, financial, and in-house research purposes. Efficient management of records is often best performed by the institution that created the original document; cultural institutions partnering with businesses for the purpose of documenting a community would do well to collaborate with this in mind. Some institutions may value the records for institutional use alone, while others might recognize and promote their worth and use beyond their walls. Archivists can encourage institutions to see the multiple values of their records. Governments, corporations, and medical facilities are just a few examples of institutional Archives. Nonprofit cultural institutions such as art museums also fit into this category.

Sometimes, the individuals managing the collections of a repository and the types of records found there may be different from what one would expect, but the accommodations benefit their care. For example, some town governments collect the papers of their residents in addition to civil records.

Those maintaining archival resources sometimes must make do with the expertise they have at hand and the monetary resources that are available. Without the

### Professional Care of Archives

This list defines the organizations that care for historical records, the types of records they generally handle, and the types of people who commonly manage them. It is intended to give a broad overview of the care of archival resources.

| Professional Repositories Handling Archives | Types of Records | Cultural Heritage Collaborator |
|---|---|---|
| University Archives/ Special Collections | Administrative documents, personal papers | Archivists, librarians |
| Town Government | Government documents | Town clerks, archivists |
| Corporations | Administrative documents (sometimes personal papers of organization's founder) | Archivists, librarians, secretaries, administrators |
| Historical Society/ Museum/Library | Personal papers, administrative documents | Curators, archivists, librarians, volunteers |

assistance of an "ideal" cultural heritage collaborator, institutions can prepare available personnel through consultants and training programs, while working toward hiring a full-time person with the expertise and time to coordinate a complete archives management program.[11] Records that wind up in a facility that differs from those in the chart on page 21 are in danger of being assigned a secondary status to the institution's other resources and functions, often not receiving the care they need or deserve. If an institution chooses to manage archives, it must be prepared to give them proper care or else endanger a piece of cultural heritage.

Historical records should be valued by diverse cultural institutions for their capacity to reveal more about our artifacts and publications than the exclusive study of those materials alone. For example, a museum that primarily collects objects benefits from the written records about those objects -— sales records, artists statements, trails of provenance, etc. Records assist with all aspects of museum management, from administrative activities to exhibition. Within a library, archival collections support the administrative function and the sense of community the institution provides to its given audience. Local history records in library collections elicit a sense of place, belonging, and a research atmosphere.

Some collecting repositories proactively seek collections and employ the use of collecting policies to further their goals. However, many (if not most) personal papers and institutional collections are lost because those who create or keep them do not recognize their historical value. Many institutions work to establish active programs to create documentation in areas that are believed to be

---

11. For example, the Gloucester City Archives is a town government Archives run in large part by volunteers. For more information about how they successfully manage their archives, see Model 4 in this book.

undocumented or under-documented. These can be quite beneficial, but many times they develop such programs without regard to true collection needs or true community documentation practices. When a repository neglects its outreach role, it threatens its collecting role and minimizes its overall purpose. We must collect thoughtfully and raise awareness of the importance of archives among those who create records so that they save what is important for posterity. Thoughtful and proactive collecting — "[k]eeping a good lookout...prowling like a wolf for prey" — helps an organization create a collection that better reflects its community.[12]

Cultural heritage organizations house historical records that were often acquired through serendipity. These are the materials that are often placed on the doorstep of the local historical society when owners have no idea where else to bring them. Every archivist has experience with this type of collection. We must evaluate the value of retaining such material. We must determine if we collect it because it is an important resource for documenting history, or if we collect it because this type of resource is easily obtained. The sources we collect must reflect a specific goal of documenting society. According to Hans Boom:

> [Our collecting function] *"has undergone a qualitative transformation in the last generation of archivists. Originally it consisted of collecting or preserving more or less sparsely and randomly retained 'leftovers.' Then, as the volume of material with the potential of forming part of the documentary heritage began to exceed the limits of what could be physically incorporated into that documentary heritage, this function changed to*

---

12. Jeremy Belknap quoted in *Documenting Localities* creates an eye-opening analogy to describe the role of the archivist in collection development.

> *comprise mainly the acquisition and preservation of materials chosen more or less thoughtfully from an overabundant store.... And, as life in our modern industrial society becomes more diverse, with its technocratic structures and its technological development problems, the mountain of data competing for storage also begins to grow at a more rapid pace."*[13]

There must be a purpose to what we do and not just a random "reactive" accumulation of materials.[14] Records are lost over time due to this approach. Many archives caretakers do not recognize the tragedy of their inactivity in this area. If we are collecting to document culture — shedding light on the broadest reaches of society possible, retaining community memory, providing evidence of human activity — our collecting must be active and not approached with casual accessioning of whatever items just happen to come our way. We must purposefully define our collecting focus and determine if our collecting strategy is based on geographic locality or a specific subject of import to our institution.

"In the past, archivists collected, and were grateful for, whatever they could find — whatever items had survived. Archivist David Gracy stated that 'the traditional approach of setting up a repository to collect like a vacuum cleaner within a given geographical area is unrealistic for twentieth-century material.'"[15] This is particularly

---

13. Hans Booms, "Society and the Formation of a Documentary Heritage: Issues in the Appraisal of Archival Sources," translated from German in *Archivaria* 24 (Summer 1987): 76.
14. Richard Cox and others promoting a community documentation theory describe this "reactive" role archivists have undertaken as opposed to the active role that they should take (*Documenting Localities*, 27).
15. Faye Phillips, "Developing Collecting Policies for Manuscript Collections," *The American Archivist* 47.1 (Winter 1984): 31, quoting David B. Gracy II, "Starting an Archives," *Georgia Archives* 1 (Fall 1972): 23-24.

important for contemporary materials, at a time when information is even more prolific in the twenty-first century due to new technologies and new ways of living that generate extensive documents. If we collect everything that comes across our path without discerning which materials actually benefit our mission, we cannot expect to facilitate adequate access with complete finding aids that emphasize collections' strengths. Operating as stand-alone repositories, we cannot expect to have the time to collect, appraise, arrange, preserve, and describe archival material that is not central to our goals. For this reason, we must be more discriminating when filling our storage areas.

Furthermore, we must understand that the collections we aim to acquire are most valuable in certain forms. With this in mind, professional archival repositories aim to collect "natural collections" of large groups of records. Such collections keep their original order and reflect the thought processes of the records' creators. The ideal of retaining the arrangement of a collection is called "sanctity of original order." In general, natural collections are donated by one person or by an institution and possess a clear origin (known as "provenance" or "*respect de fonds*") that helps confirm the records' authenticity and ensures that records by different creators remain distinct. Full collections tell us more about the records' origins, subject, and, ultimately, history than individual pieces of paper or collections that are "artificially arranged" by intermingling distinct groups of records.[16]

Artificial arrangement is when an organizational method is imposed by the archivist who prepares the records for housing in the repository. It should be avoided whenever possible and only used when collections arrive thoroughly jumbled or are not accessioned as part of full

---

16. More thorough definitions of archival terms can be found in the glossary section of this book.

collections. Too often, collections are broken up and reorganized, removing their integrity for research and evidential purposes. Small historical societies tend to artificially arrange individual items by separating them from collections accessioned intact to form subject-based arrangements of materials. This goes against basic tenets of professional archives management that require organizations to retain a collection as it is to ensure that the intent of its creator is maintained. Imposing a subjective thematic arrangement can destroy any useful information that the initial order provided. A processor may think the arrangement is unimportant and unintentionally destroy valuable inherent value by rearranging.

Only when no original order is present should an archivist seek to apply one, creating an artificial arrangement of records that attempts to re-create a sense of the records' purpose. The artificial arrangement should make the subject or creator of the collection more understandable or immediate. The act of artificial arrangement imposes a bias on the records, subjecting them to the interpretation of the archivist rather than displaying the thoughts of those directly involved in an event or activity. For example, records related to a company that are gathered by a staff member will show us the day-to-day activities of the organization and perhaps the attitudes of one directly involved with events. Individual pieces of paper that are chosen and arranged by the archivist in a collection would likely be more prominent documents that tell us what the arranger knows about an organization based on her own research and analysis.

In addition to primary sources created and organized by the originator of a collection, archival repositories also sometimes include secondary sources and ephemera, though these types of materials are not officially called "archives." Secondary sources refer to nonoriginal, mass-produced materials such as photocopies and published items (e.g., news clippings, books, and articles). This information may be rearranged without qualm by the archivist when it holds no useful creator order.[17] In general, secondary sources are materials that were produced by someone who was not present when the event occurred — either separated by space or time. Some secondary-source items or artifacts not normally considered archival could be housed in an Archives because of some special characteristic. For example, a bible would generally be part of a library collection and not an archival collection, but a family bible that has handwritten family data in it includes original information that may be important to an Archives. Secondary sources are also useful for research purposes in the Archives to provide interpretative information.

Ephemera include ticket stubs, brochures, invitations, and other materials that are short-lived in nature. They are materials that are not intended to last forever but were created en masse for a specific, one-time purpose. This purpose can include publicity for an event or the dissemination of timely information to educate the public. Ephemera are often housed with archival material because their transient nature can make the material rare. Like archives, ephemera are produced as part of, or as a reflection of, an event or activity.

Thoughtful evaluation of the types of resources we collect and our reasons for doing so allows us to better care for our archival collections. With a better understanding of the nature of archives in general, we are prepared to form a solid foundation for the improvement of these holdings within our own repositories. Using tools to assist with collection development and planning, we can become adept at gathering resources that preserve society's knowledge

---

17. Some news clippings and other published materials are considered to be primary sources when observers of an event wrote them. In some cases, there is a fine line between what is considered primary and what is considered secondary.

and community identity, rather than just collecting for the sake of gathering interesting materials that perhaps hold intrinsic value, but have little informational value. Using mindful means to gather materials helps prevent society from losing historical resources due to neglect, allowing us to better explain our role to our community and preparing us to work collaboratively to form a complete documentary record of our locales. "Archivists have to understand, accept, and work within the reality that we — through our selection — through our marketing — do as much to create the documentation of the past as the individuals and organizations that generated the records in the first place."[18]

The thoughts and activities of our ancestors are conveyed for posterity in the archival records that they left behind. Archives validate or invalidate our thoughts about the intentions of our predecessors. Similarly, the documents that we create will explain our own ideas to our descendants. As primary sources, written at the time events occur by participants in the activities, archives serve as testament to truth and help historians evaluate views of history and changing societies. Along with artifacts and published material, archives serve as a prime element for greater understanding of civilization. As materials that are collected and created by all organizations regardless of function, archives form the backbone of cultural understanding.

---

18. Mark A. Green, "The Power of Archives: Archivists' Values and Value in the Postmodern Age," *The American Archivist* 72 (Spring/Summer 2009): 25.

**The Snowball Effect**

Grass-roots efforts to value archives can build an effective documentation program. The following shows the momentum that can be built by starting small, staying focused, and proceeding one step at a time.

- acknowledge the need to pay more attention to documentation and archives
- seek to give proper care to archives within the community
- search for cultural heritage partners
- work to better understand collections and their potential through surveys and collection development
- secure more resources to manage collections
- provide better outreach
- encourage more people to use collections
- attract more volunteers
- gain greater support from community based on appearance of competence and early successes
- demonstrate need for better preservation and facilities
- increase ability to handle more collections
- document more complete community history

## How the Care of Archives Differs from Artifacts and Books

The main conceptual areas where archives are fundamentally different from artifact and book collections are important to recognize for the purposes of processing and general care. These areas include:

- Sanctity of original order — Archives or Special collections are generally acquired in groupings of papers from an institution or individual. If the archives creator ascribes an order to a collection, an archivist must do her best to maintain that order. The arrangement of collections focuses on large groupings of records called record groups (fonds), series, and subseries. Archival documents are not accessioned one record at a time, nor are they arranged or described one item at a time (except in unique circumstances). This differs from both books and artifacts.

- Provenance, or respect de fonds — The place where archives originated and the creator of the documents are important in determining the uniqueness, authenticity, and proper arrangement of records. This is similar to artifacts but possesses little importance for most book collections (except in the case of rare books).

- Appraisal — In the world of archives, appraisal refers to the process of determining whether or not documents should be kept. Appraisal guidelines are set through collecting policies to help archivists determine whether or not whole collections should be accessioned into the repository. It is also performed as an archivist "processes" a collection — arranging, preserving, and describing materials — determining if individual documents add value to the collection or should be discarded. Appraisal to most librarians and curators would mean determining monetary value.

- Finding aids — Collections are described using various guides and indices with specialized formats that highlight elements such as the scope of the collection and biographical information about the author. They can also include detailed information about collection contents. Information can be placed in electronic databases using standardized systems created specifically for archives management. To describe large groupings of materials rather than individual items, a finding aid must contain multiple layers of description that fit materials into context, unlike item-level descriptions used for books and artifacts. Archivists, museum professionals, and librarians use their own standards for electronically describing information about collections, but they often overlap. Attempts are being made to bring together diverse descriptive efforts, especially in university and large repository settings.

---

## Why Value Archives?

- To better understand a society, its people, and their activities
- To provide primary information about society's activities to help citizenry and scholars recognize and evaluate these events for themselves, so that they may discern truth and reality from fiction and biases
- To support an accurate and diverse documentary record of human existence and human action
- To foster a sense of community and to strengthen civic pride based on a shared and documented history
- To provide support for understanding the community and how communities form the building blocks of state, national, and global societies
- To evaluate the role a community played in historical events on a state, national, or international scale
- To ensure administrative continuity as organizations and businesses function and evolve
- To ensure a smooth-running society governed with order and efficiency
- To hold public officials accountable with organized public records that can be viewed by citizenry
- To help ensure freedom
- To hold liable those who stifle mores, repress societies, and otherwise degrade human rights
- To secure property rights and provide evidence of ownership
- To provide evidence against those who break laws

- To make materials available for review for assistance with planning, allowing us to avoid repeating the mistakes of the past and to focus on the successful ideas of others that have been committed to record
- To promote efficiency in records management programs by distinguishing materials with long-term evidential, informational, and historical value
- To promote the study of a town or organization to researchers
- To market a community and promote tourism using a deep knowledge about the community's history and strengths
- To recognize and support the links among all institutions and individuals that create and collect documents in society
- To evaluate society and distinguish trends from more permanent traits of diversified culture
- To support the provenance and documentation of collections of objects
- To support the management of secondary-source collections such as those found in a library
- To support and supplement public education and lifelong learning
- To serve as illustrative works for educational, cultural, and other diversified programming
- To preserve cherished memories of family, friends, and community
- To define one's own identity and have some reassurance of one's continued memory through personal documentation

---

## Model 1

## Using Archives to Support Collections:

### The Wenham Museum

"The Mission of the Wenham Museum is to protect, preserve, and interpret the history and culture of Boston's North Shore, domestic life, and the artifacts of childhood."[19] The prime focus of the museum is its collection of toys (most notably, its dolls and trains), textiles, and the circa 1690 Claflin-Richards House. Making use of its artifacts, the museum displays remarkable permanent exhibits and also tends rotating exhibits of outside sources that relate to its institutional mission.

The Wenham Museum is an outstanding example of an organization focusing on its collections to drive its core mission. The holdings of the museum are extensive. Within the collections policy is a statement of the museum's vision "to interpret the domestic lives, the regional culture, and the broader influences of the residents of Wenham and the North Shore." Staff use their collections to "explore the artifacts and history of families and childhood, of daily life, and events which impact the people of the North Shore. Museum staff and volunteers teach and maintain the skills and traditions of the past to today's families." The collection policy also highlights the library holdings, archives, and educational items that are used for hands-on study.

---

19. Quotes on this page are from the Wenham Museum's collections policy and Web site (www.wenhammuseum.org).

The Wenham Museum is the only of its sort in Massachusetts. And while it does not currently work directly with outside organizations for collection development matters, it seeks to stand out in a crowd of local history museums with its unique focus. The museum recognizes how each type of collection supports another with the cultural resources of artifacts, books, and archives working together to reflect their community and subject focus. To this end, the museum is working on refining policy to more clearly define its niche and describe how its diverse materials relate to each other and to the collections of their neighboring institutions.

The museum resides within the Town of Wenham (pop. 4,600). The historic Claflin-Richards House that was purchased in 1922 "by the philanthropic Wenham Village Improvement Society for the purpose of preservation and exhibition." A former resident of the house donated her 800-item historic doll collection soon thereafter to begin the institution's permanent collection. The museum is now a small, professionally run organization that was incorporated in 1952 and first accredited by the AAM (American Association of Museums) in 1973. It retains a staff of approximately 15 employees, including curators, educators, and other specialists in the areas of finance, membership, publicity, and office and shop management. The museum also coordinates about 50 regular volunteers.

In support of the artifacts and hands-on educational mission of the institution, the Wenham Museum maintains a library collection of approximately 100 linear feet of books. Most of these books relate to the care and history of dolls and toys; others relate to the local history of Wenham. Within the museum building is a room for the storage of archival material. The archives primarily relate to the local history of the area, with extensive photographic collections. The archives also include ledgers, greeting and trade cards, maps, scrapbooks, institutional records, genealogies, pamphlets, clippings, and some local records on loan. These collections are often used for exhibit or to generate exhibit ideas. The museum staff is seeking money to perform a survey of the archival materials to evaluate their overall role within the organization's larger collecting goals.

Archives often play a supporting role within their institution, as is evidenced at the Wenham Museum. Careful control and maintenance of archival resources can greatly benefit an institution by providing it with desirable research material and fascinating fodder for exhibits. Wenham stands as a model for institutions of all sorts seeking to gain control of their cultural collections and collection development. As the Wenham Museum seeks to refine its role, it more easily will be able to reach out to potential collaborators, make its own collections stronger, play a leading role in documenting a specific aspect of its community, and make itself more visible to potential donors and supporters. Focusing on collection management is a smart way to strengthen any cultural heritage institution.

# 2. Collection Development and Collaboration

The safekeeping of archives ensures that knowledge of our past and present culture is preserved for future generations. Chapter One explained why it is important to identify, collect, organize, preserve, and provide access to the archival materials that make up the documentary record. Coordinated efforts to accomplish these tasks enable us to, on a large scale, systematically gather records with enduring value. This chapter will provide detailed information about collaborative collecting within a given community, whether that community is geographically based or subject-based.

Outreach is a vital component of a healthy cultural institution. In an age when society is linked globally through computers, people expect easy accessibility to information. An institution that tries to go it alone, without linking to other institutions in some way, will be lost and will become obsolete. To reach out to others effectively, an institution must work to develop a collection development policy that keeps the collection goals of neighboring institutions in mind. This chapter defines the need for planned and coordinated collecting strategies with suggestions for how to accomplish them.

We should begin the development of our collecting strategies with the idea that collecting should be diverse and spread among numerous repositories to encompass the broad range of human knowledge. Biased and unplanned collecting of resources is a danger to the creation of a truly reflective documentary record. Record collections are most often gathered and created based on an individual institution's desires and the ready availability of records related to those in society who are most visible. Without knowing the extent of available materials, institutions request items from those in their circle or from well-known characters in town, taking whatever is given by them and not looking beyond that which is offered. This generally works to guarantee the easy availability of certain types of records and can obscure a well-rounded presentation of a history that represents a full and complete view of an era.

The problem does not reside fully with the collector. The push by researchers to locate records related to their particular research topic often encourages archivists to seek collections that help an exclusive group of patrons. Similarly, administrators often push archivists to accession collections that will bring prominence to the institution, seeking the records of well-known individuals rather than records that fulfill a particular collecting function. There are strategies to avoid this — from the creation of collecting policies to the use of reference statistics to show what diverse users are seeking at an institution. Reference statistics can guide the repository toward strengthening subject areas already valued by varied audiences. Statistics show which materials are most highly used as well as those that are sought by patrons but are not found among collections. When appropriate, archivists can use this information to strengthen areas where researchers show interest.

As discussed in the previous chapter, a repository must aim to fill a documentation gap with records reflecting all points of view of a subject, rather than just those that reflect the popular view or the perspective that just happened to be captured on paper. The documentation of history must offer "multiple perspectives on enduring concerns."[20] All records are subjective, demonstrating the viewpoints of their creators. History is not always fact, but it is an interpretation of past events. It is the role of the archivist to provide the diverse primary-source materials necessary to think about and better understand the present day and preceding eras by establishing collection criteria consistent with a defined mission. Focused collections with diverse viewpoints and a potential for growth should form the backbone of any cultural heritage institution.

Popular views and ones that are often the most visible in society seem weighted toward one perspective or another. The archivist must try to look objectively at civilization to determine what materials are needed to reflect all aspects of it. Some collections are saved only by virtue of the status of their creators. While records about well-known people are certainly sought by institutions, in many cases they are also pushed onto them. While the manuscripts of lesser-known individuals are often ignored or destroyed before they can be given to an Archives, the average individual does not realize how his records may be beneficial for a repository. An archivist must strive to overcome these challenges. Similarly, corporations that value their recorded history and those that have the monetary resources to preserve it are usually better represented in archival repositories than lesser-known businesses. This "documentary residue" does not provide an all-inclusive collective memory of a culture and instead perpetuates a biased view of history. Archives that do not actively seek materials with a goal of creating balanced collections generally are gathering only the most available resources and are therefore not living up to a role as objective keepers of the primary documents of history.

---

20. Archibald, 166.

> *While the maintenance of government accountability and administrative continuity, and the protection of personal rights, are still rightly recognized as important purposes for archives, the principal justification for archives to most users, and to the tax-paying public at large, as also reflected in most national and state archival legislation, rests on archives being able to offer citizens a sense of identity, locality, history, culture, and personal and collective memory. Simply stated, it is no longer acceptable to limit the definition of society's memory solely to the documentary residue left over (or chosen) by powerful record creators. Public and historical accountability demands more of archives, and of archivists.*[21]

Do you worry that if you do not take in an archival collection it will disappear? Do you often think that your institution is the only place that might be interested in a resource and therefore you must "save" it? Do you try to imagine how a potential donation will fit among your collections without written guidelines to assist your decision-making? Do you collect archives because you think no one else in town does? Planning is the key to overcoming these challenges.

A well-known way of collecting in many institutions is when materials are dropped on the front stoop of the repository. Without planning, organizations are more likely to accept anything offered to them. Fearful that valuable historical resources will be destroyed if they turn away materials, organizations tend to accept inappropriate items. Sometimes organizations are equally fearful that

---

21. Terry Cook, "Archival Science and Postmodernism: New Formulations for Old Concepts," *Archival Science* 1.1 (2000): 3–24. Text available at http://www.mybestdocs.com/cook-t-postmod-p1-00.htm.

they will not get further donations if they turn away any materials, but "sporadic, unplanned, competitive, and overlapping manuscript collecting has led to the growth of poor collections of marginal value."[22]

To develop valuable collections that do not leave gaps in the documentary record, an archivist must be an active participant in collecting resources that are interpretive of society rather than just a passive collector of any documents that come his way. Within their policies, archivists must evaluate and write about their collecting role to ensure that they are assisting the documentary record and the efficient preservation of their community's resources. "While total inclusion is an ideal and not an attainable goal, active efforts will result in a narrative that encompasses more perspectives and consequently represents more people and a greater consensus about the meaning of the past and the possibilities for the future."[23]

Reaching out directly to those who create records, educating them about the importance of their materials, and encouraging them to preserve their point of view in archival repositories is a vital component of our efforts. Repositories must encourage individuals to preserve and document family history to help preserve the day-to-day activities that help define a larger history of our city, state, and country. Similarly, archivists must encourage businesses and associations of all sizes to preserve their records and recognize their importance to society. You may ask potential donors to consider the records in their possession that may have importance to other citizens and explain the value that personal papers have to a wide variety of people. When appropriate, cultural heritage caretakers should also encourage record creators to donate

---

22. Faye Phillips, "Developing Collecting Policies for Manuscript Collections," *The American Archivist* (Winter 1984).
23. Archibald, 156.

materials to a local collecting repository. Striving to match records to particular repositories that best suit their needs and where they can fill an appropriate documentation role, archivists should be able to turn to mission statements and collecting policies for guidance.

**Some Types of Researchers Who Visit Archives**

- Scholars studying history or trends in society
- Students writing papers
- Genealogists and individuals interested in family history
- Professionals such as engineers interested in land or building development
- Government officials interested in learning constituents and promoting community
- Homeowners interested in house histories or technical information about their home construction
- Marketers seeking nostalgic materials related to their business to use in campaigns
- Reporters seeking evidence and information about the past to use in articles
- Business owners looking for old photographs and documents to decorate their buildings
- Documentary writers and show producers seeking materials to illustrate their work
- Individuals involved in legal battles related to varied issues who are seeking documents to support their case

In the end, to properly accomplish the task of documenting society, repositories must work together to actively pursue appropriate resources from the variety of those available. There is a "need to change our perspective, from our egocentric need to build up our own archival institutions to a common concern to build up information linkages between institutions."[24] The goal of cooperative collection development is to enable organizations to establish a specific focus in order that they may play a particular collecting role in the archival community, aiming to work with partners to keep a record of society in its entirety. Cooperative collection development will help ensure that all aspects of history are being adequately documented, and that the broad base of human knowledge is spread among collaborative repositories. Working together will ensure that cultural organizations are playing an appropriate role in maintaining archives and not spreading themselves beyond the scope of their mission.

Cooperation enables institutions to fill a specific documentation gap so the history of a particular topic and as many different views of that subject as possible are preserved. By focusing attention on the completeness of the documentary record related to a particular issue, a repository meets its need to reflect diverse knowledge, while opening the doors for other repositories to fill other known gaps in the historical evidence. This view encourages the archives-collecting function of the smallest museum to hold as much importance as the role of a large university Archives. When everyone has a responsibility, collecting is efficient. The idea of pursuing a specific collecting strategy allows collection development to move from the theoretical or ideological to the practical for everyone. It helps the implementation of a collections policy become a logical and necessary part of the institution's functioning. It eliminates the idea of collecting on an expansive scale, which often creates an

---

24. Gerald Ham quoted in Faye Phillips, "Developing Collection Development Policies for Manuscript Collections," *The American Archivist* 471 (Winter 1984): 35.

overwhelming sense of community responsibility and an unrealistic expectation of the organization's purpose.

It is the archival repositories' duty to try to make sure no one is being left out of history due to the absence of a collecting strategy. It is not any one institution's task to take it all on alone. Each repository should work collaboratively with others to define the collecting roles of individuals in the archives community. Together, they can compare goals and create guidelines to better document history on a large scale. Opening discussions with other institutions while writing collection development policies allows organizations to define themselves and document the history of a community, country, and culture more effectively. It makes it easier to collect materials, allowing the various repositories to state explicitly what items they are trying to locate as differentiated from others. Each institution should distinguish itself from its partners by tying its archives-collecting goals to its mission statement and by focusing its policy on a particular piece of the documentary record. Lacking a policy for collecting, institutions generally try to collect too broadly, leaving gaps in their collections and in the documentation of society. Organizations that try to collect in the same areas in which others are collecting will compete for resources, gathering incomplete series of information that have limited use.

The ramifications of missing pieces of information in our repositories extend beyond the weakened collections themselves. A collections policy is one of the primary tools cultural organizations have to reach out to the public. Planning for an organization's future, including the creation of a collection development policy, is important to ensure that the organization has a clear direction with a strong set of resources for organizational development. The policy must define how archives fit among all collections, including those of artifacts and books. Clearly defined goals, and strategies for reaching them, along with measurements implemented to ensure the success of attaining goals, are important to keep an organization healthy. Policies help prevent confusion about basic institutional tenets: They help staff work together, facilitate relationships with donors, and attract users to collections.

An organization that collects collaboratively and thoughtfully will have a better and more focused collection, which will allow it to provide better services to its constituents. No individual institution can collect everything: Instead, a focused collection policy will enable an institution to be stronger in a particular area than it could ever possibly be with a broad, ill-defined collecting base. Collaborative collecting encourages repositories to refer donations suitable for partners to the appropriate repository. Such focus also allows the institution to better market to appropriate potential users and to design activities of particular relevance to the collections and those interested in them. A clear collection development policy stating what your institution collects and what it does not collect will assist researchers by making it easier for them to know where to go to find the materials they seek.

Every department within a particular organization has a particular function. Similarly, every repository collecting archives plays a particular role in documenting history. Working together, they make stronger collections than working separately, with each repository relying on another to help tell the story of civilization, and each representing a stronger piece of a larger whole. Those working toward filling a gap in the documentary record solidify their importance as a protector of a selected piece of human knowledge.

## Reaching Out for Partners

Considering the development or rewriting of a collecting strategy provides an institution with an ideal opportunity for establishing a collaborative group. Those developing local collections should meet with colleagues to find out what other institutions in the geographic region are collecting and form their own collecting goals. Individuals should make contacts with government repositories, record agencies (businesses and universities), and special collections that one may not have considered as partners but who may still be collecting similar records.[25] This section assumes that you recognize the need for collection development and are considering collaborative work. It aims to assist with forming a collaborative group and helps you overcome challenges associated with cooperative projects.

A collaboration is a formal understanding between partners that announces they will work together to create something that is different from what they had when working alone. Collaboration brings together individuals that have something in common, yet have differing expertise and viewpoints. "Collaboration anchors not in the process of relationship, but in the pursuit of a specific result. Collaboratives are established to solve problems, develop new understandings, design new products."[26] A cultural heritage collaborative designed around collection development recognizes a need to better identify available historical resources, to establish unique collecting goals for

---

25. See section on the Community Documentation Strategy for more information on identifying collaborative partners.
26. Leo Denise. "Collaboration vs. C-Three (Cooperation, Coordination, and Communication)," *Innovating*.

repositories, and to work together to promote collections and subsequent collection-related programs and activities for the public. Collaboration is a strategy to achieve the end result of better planned collections, resulting in better community documentation, the creation of better access tools and greater public awareness/participation in the activities of cultural heritage institutions.[27]

Related to collaboration are coordination and cooperation. Both are useful in establishing a collaborative, but they can be pursued separately from one. Coordination is the creation of a partnership to promote efficiency. In the cultural heritage fields, coordination can help organizations avoid collection overlap and competition for resources, but it does not assume that partners will work together beyond that. Cooperation does not even involve partnering, but instead encourages organizations to recognize that they are both part of a community and therefore should work together amicably. For example, if a repository is offered a donation that does not fit into its collecting scope, it would cooperatively refer it to another more appropriate organization. Cooperation and coordination can be beneficial in collaboration, but they are not comprehensive strategies for achieving long-term, focused results.

If we choose to pursue a long-term partnering strategy, we first must recognize that a successful collaborative is required, to some extent, to put the needs of the collaborative above those of individual institutions. This is not to say that you must abandon the goals of your own organization. In fact, a successful collaborative will meld with an individual institution's own ideals. When entering a collaborative, you make a formal agreement to

---

27. For related information regarding the stages of collaboration and elements of successful project partnerships, see Alexandra Yarrow, Barbara Clubb, and Jennifer-Lynn Draper's "Public Libraries, Archives and Museums: Trends in Collaboration and Cooperation," IFLA Professional Reports, 108. International Federation of Library Associations and Institutions (2008): 32–34.

adhere to the principles established by the collective. Individuals must also recognize that they will need to dedicate some time toward collaborative work. This means that participants must be willing to take some time away from other projects to devote attention to group-related cooperative tasks.

The more devoted the group, the more focused its members will become and the better they can manage their collecting goals and outreach initiatives. The voices of many advocating for archives are louder than those of individual institutions trying to garner separate support. A group professing similar principles will raise more awareness than an individual espousing those ideals.

The first step toward establishing a collaborative is to carefully reach out to prospective partners and plan for the development of a partnership based on mutual agreement. Those with the initiative to start a group must carefully consider what they want the group to achieve. "For a collaborative idea to succeed, it has to be embedded in an overarching vision all participants share, which makes it worth the effort to overcome the inevitable obstacles."[28]

Partners must recognize possible pitfalls before they occur. Whether you seek to establish a formal incorporated group or an informal group, there are basic procedures to encourage its success. Partnerships are often unsuccessful due to miscommunication, insufficient planning, or setting unachievable goals. "Collaboration, as a human enterprise, totally depends for its success upon the goodwill of its participants."[29] The group must work to communicate and keep everyone informed of intentions and developments as the collaborative proceeds. The group must also be sure to

---

28. Diane M. Zorich, Gunter Waibel, and Ricky Erway, *Beyond the Silos of the LAMs: Among Library, Archives and Museums* (Dublin, OH: OCLC, 2008), 21.
29. James Burgett. *Collaborative Collection Development: A Practical Guide for Your Library* (Chicago: ALA, 2004), 23.

plan activities by creating formal written documents describing goals and objectives that are created with the input of all group members. Though much of the information provided in this section may seem obvious, it is important to highlight it and outline ways to advance step-by-step to achieve goals. Many groups are derailed because of simple misunderstandings, lack of initial planning, and failure to commit ideas to paper.

To recognize that conflicting personalities, old hard feelings, and other obstacles must sometimes be overcome for collaborating individuals to work well together, members must acknowledge differences and past mistakes or disagreements and put them aside for the group to progress. Competition for resources is often one of the largest areas for misunderstanding. To successfully collaborate, institutions must agree to put competition aside for the good of the community and for the long-range goal of building strong individual collections and a solid community documentary record. The development of thoughtful collecting policies requires flexibility from all parties and will assist with building strong partnerships, as well as solid historical documentation. "Successful collaborations don't require friendship or even that the collaborators like one another very much. Like competence, however, there must be a minimum threshold of mutual respect, tolerance, and trust for a collaboration to succeed. Successful collaborators tend to ignore the more irritating quirks and idiosyncrasies of their colleagues. They focus on managing one another's strengths rather than one another's lesser qualities."[30]

A collaborative group should begin with a focus on easily achievable goals that guide everyone in the same direction. Long-range planning can be initiated once the

---

30. Michael Schrage, "The Rules of Collaboration," *Indiana Libraries* 18.3–4 (1999): 1.

group is running efficiently. The committee must create milestones that, once reached, serve as a measure of the group's success. A primary goal is to encourage a cooperative ethic that will lead to efficiency and increased access to expertise in a wide range of fields.

To begin a collaborative, one individual must assume responsibility to be the driving force toward its initial development. "A project must be designed, implemented, and managed by people who have the skills, background, and resources to make it a priority and a success. Because they bear the responsibility for ensuring that the project progresses, they must be granted the authority to listen and respond to concerns of participants, make course adjustments as necessary, and scale the project to the level of participants' commitment."[31]

The leader should try to make a personal connection with targeted partners. Aim to contact people one-on-one by telephone or personally visit those maintaining archives to announce the intention to establish a cooperative group. To be taken seriously, you must be armed with information that explains the value of archives, why such a group is needed to care for them, what a collaborative can do to help the town, and how it can help individual members. You should proceed with care. People invited to initial cooperative meetings often misunderstand intentions and feel that the initiator is trying to immediately centralize resources and take their collections away from them. Being aware of this potential hurdle can help you avoid it. The group initiator must be confident and prepared to explain the benefits of collaboration. He must keep everyone focused and express the need for long-term commitment and determination. "...committed and consistent leadership

---

31. Burgett, 47.

is probably the best predictor of [collaborative] sustainability."[32]

As an initiator tries to bring together collaborators, he may find that there are people unwilling to participate at the outset. As the group flourishes, interest in the collaborative will grow. Just as there will be disinterest, there will also be individuals who are excited about the possibilities that such a collaborative can bring. These individuals can create a foundation for future success.

The group should plan to first meet on a date and time that works for the most people who demonstrate interest in the project. So, when people are first contacted, the organizer must be sure to ask them about what times would work best for their schedules. Plan to hold the initial meeting in a comfortable space, such as the meeting room at the local library. Try to choose a neutral place that will not make anyone feel uncomfortable. Send out written invitations to the meeting a few weeks in advance; include the date, time, location, and a brief agenda reiterating that the purpose of collaborating is to share information about collections. Send reminder notices or call to confirm a couple of days before the event. It can be helpful to ask participants for comments before the group meeting, so that their comments can be used anonymously to prompt conversation if members are reticent at the meeting itself.

At the first meeting, the person who organized the event should be a facilitator who seeks the opinions of others; he must try not to take center stage for the duration of the meeting. The facilitator may wish to reiterate the purpose of the meeting at the outset and then immediately open the floor to others. Once the organizer reiterates the benefits of establishing a collaborative for archives collection development and management, ask others to

---

32. Burgett, 78.

name additional benefits they perceive. Write these ideas down. Brainstorm possible goals for the group that will generate enthusiasm. For example, plan to work on collection development policies or identify cooperative exhibition projects that highlight extant collections and that will generate initial enthusiasm. Ask someone to take minutes at each meeting. This will keep groups organized and moving ahead with plans. If no one speaks up with ideas, and no one volunteers for minute-taking or other necessary tasks, the facilitator must step in and gently prod people for information and encourage more active participation. This person should also be sure to volunteer her own time to any agreed-upon activities so that others can see she is willing to do what she asks of them.

At the initial meeting, get contact information for everyone in the group (make sure that everyone lists more than one way that they can be reached). If possible, make copies of the attendance list at the meeting or mail copies to participants after the event. Set up a date and time for the next meeting and try to establish a tentative agenda. Plan to hold monthly meetings at a regularly scheduled time to keep the group active, and provide people with tasks and deadlines. Type meeting minutes immediately following the session: Distribute them to everyone in the group and to collection managers who did not attend the meeting. A formal agenda should be sent out with reminder notices for the next meeting (meetings without agendas tend to last longer than they should and waste time). These agendas should be mailed out at least a week ahead of the event so that people can avoid filling their calendars with other commitments.

Do not schedule excessive meetings. Rather, get the most out of monthly meetings by sticking to an agenda. Establish a group leader who may or may not be the original person who worked to get the group established. The discussion leader can be changed for each meeting, or one person can be elected for this role. If there is no facilitator, you may find that the group has difficulty staying on topic. The person guiding the discussion can also ensure that everyone's views are heard. As the group grows, they may also seek individuals for specific committee work such as publicity and programming.

Those who work directly with archives will form the core group that launches goals for the collaborative. Outside participants who have an interest in history and culture should then be invited to help elaborate upon the goals and to implement them. Everyone may have different ideas about where the collaborative should head. Try to focus on the similarities to begin with rather than the differences. Work to include competent individuals who will subscribe to the principles and goals of the group. The core group of collaborators must aim to create an amenable overall vision of the archives committee and should work together to steer the group toward the common established goals. All participants should be encouraged to share ideas and be made to feel as if they are an important part of the process. No one individual should be allowed to dominate or steer the committee away from common goals. Those leading the group should not dominate conversations but should work to ensure that organization members stay targeted on appropriate discussions.

Continually look for ways to have the group work together toward commonalities. Do not concentrate too heavily on one objective at the expense of other growth opportunities, and do not focus on a goal that emotionally divides the group. Work to center participants' ideology around accomplishing effective historical documentation. The first step should be to get collections in order and focused. Large outreach projects can wait until the group has been functioning smoothly and amicably for some time. First meetings should include discussion that attempts to establish common ground, set a tone for the group, and establish a structure with a mission and goals.

Dialogue about areas of disagreement should be encouraged, and the group should hear all ideas before decisions are made. Often, the more experienced members of a group will try to dominate and push their ideas on others, thinking that they are more advanced because they have been part of a collaborative before or because they have been in the field longer; they therefore think they know the best way to accomplish tasks. But every collaborative is different, and different dynamics must be acknowledged. Younger professionals and volunteers often have a new angle to contribute that improves upon old ideas. Things should not be done as they were in the past just because they previously were successful: These ideas may prove not to work in a new setting, with new personalities, at a new time. A collaborative should be flexible and work to improve on old ways. Participants may need to break common tenets. New members with different ideas garnered from alternate experiences can often help a project leap forward.

As groups grow and achieve results, they may wish to make their collaborative status more permanent through written agreements, the application of formal rules and regulations, or the pursuit of joint administration. When organizations first attempt to collaborate to care for community archival resources, they form a "joint partnership for issue advocacy."[33] They share long-term goals, are focused on the issue of documentation, incorporate varied expertise, and retain their autonomy. Formal establishment shows that the group is serious about its mission and future as a collaborative. It acknowledges

33. Arizona Board of Regents on behalf of ASU Lodestar Center for Philanthropy and Nonprofit Innovation, *Models of Collaboration: Nonprofit Organizations Working Together* (2009): 8.

that principals have set the groundwork for success through planning. Official arrangements boost visibility and fundraising efforts. They provide a foundation for collaboration beyond collection development for collaborative purchasing, programming, and other activities. More formal arrangements can lead to the development of a new organization that links partners through a new nonprofit entity. "The creation of this new organization reflects both a maturity of purpose and a desire for entrepreneurial parent organizations to push a new effort out of the nest and provide the freedom that is sometimes necessary for new social enterprises to flourish."[34]

---

34. Arizona Board of Regents, 9.

---

### Model of an Unsuccessful Collaborative

A collaborative within a small city strived to bring together a municipality's cultural heritage institutions to strengthen their presence within the community and to promote the valuable history of the municipality. Included in the collaborative were museum professionals, librarians, archivists, businessmen, town government representatives, and volunteers with subject specific knowledge and an interest in history. During the development of the collaborative, a push for tourism overshadowed collection care, leaving the town without well-established, well-planned collections that could serve as a base for promoting visitation. At the outset, this group was largely unsuccessful—their anonymous example serves to highlight some of the problems a collaborative may encounter.

- Organizers of the collaborative came in with set goals that they pushed through without discussion.
- They did not listen to people they invited to their initial meeting who had differing ideas of what the collaborative should be or could accomplish.
- They focused on the ideas of the more politically powerful and the more experienced in the group without acknowledging the diverse experiences of other group members. They allowed those with money to take over the group rather than incorporating ideas of those with an interest primarily in collections and history.
- They were wary of new people who were not raised in the town, treating them as outsiders.

- They were distrustful of new ideas and preferred the status quo.
- They were wary of each other due to past events and held on to feelings of jealousy and competitiveness. They never acknowledged these negative emotions and let them simmer as an undercurrent of hostility during group meetings.
- They put the perceived best interests of their own establishments ahead of the collaborative. They focused on how the collaborative would help their individual institutions rather than on how it would help the town and the preservation of history. This kept them from recognizing how the group would truly promote their well-being and the community in the long term.
- They showed excessive concern over who was spending the most time on collaborative projects.
- They did not understand one another's collections, did not seek to rectify this, and rather than working toward a mission that would harmonize all their strengths, they immediately set goals that created division among group members.
- Rather than starting with a focus on their collections, they immediately jumped to promoting local tourism through the promotion of their institutions. (While this is a worthwhile goal and endeavor, cultural institutions need strong collections that people will want to visit before they can promote themselves. Without a strong sense of identity and strong resources to promote, institutions cannot convince outsiders of their worth. Patrons who visit institutions with poor management and unfocused collections likely will not be impressed with what they find.)

---

## Model 2

## Collaborating to Preserve Town History: Danvers Archives

The Danvers Web page reads "Incorporated 1757 — The King unwilling," giving one some idea of this Massachusetts town's rich history. With pride, Danvers supports a centralized repository for the care of its archival materials within its public library. The facility is maintained by a professional archivist who serves as an assistant town clerk and library department head.

A centralized archival repository is one of the most ambitious forms our cross-professional collaborative efforts may take. The facility can be equipped with proper environmental controls, shelving, and security measures to ensure the safety of all community materials. The facility can accommodate for the purchase of one set of shared equipment so that each institution does not need to spend money on individual scanners, microfilm reader/printers, and the like. A centralized program can standardize the use of appropriate housing supplies and methods of storage to provide further protection for permanent materials. It increases uniform accessibility to everyone. A well-organized records center provides accurate and efficient retrieval. It allows the collaborative organizations in town to easily standardize the way records are maintained, organized, retrieved, and disposed to ensure efficiency in the way information is managed. Standardization also ensures security when proper handling, preservation, and disaster planning for all materials are implemented. Centralization facilitates organized documentation of local history: It is a highly visible way to ensure that the needs of local archives remain a priority.

The Danvers Archival Center, started in the early 1970s, encourages cooperation among all facilities holding records in Danvers. Some energetic, enthusiastic, and forward-thinking townspeople devised the idea of this collaborative archives repository. According to the archivist, rather than developing a formal documentation plan, they started their archival program with the hope that "if you build the facility, they will come." Town government and institutions were invited to place their records on permanent deposit in a safe environment, under the supervision of a professional.[35]

Preceding the development of the Archives, an archaeological project raised awareness about history in Danvers, which helped citizens understand the importance of documenting their history and saving their historical records. Outreach work is continually performed by the archivist to demonstrate the importance of maintaining archival resources. Early on in the Archives development, one of the local churches with important records related to the infamous Salem witch trials was convinced by archives proponents that the new facility would be an ideal place to keep their holdings. Other churches and town institutions joined the collaborative when they realized that the church with such important records was willing to take part.

The success of the Danvers program is due to the single-mindedness of key people to ensure that the Archives came to fruition. Success begat more success, and now, thirty years since its inception, the Archival Center gets more acquisitions than it has ever before in its history. Few towns in New England centralize such extensive public and private holdings in one repository, under the control of one professional. Danvers serves as a model of the benefits of perseverance and centralization.

---

35. Based on author's conversation and e-mails with Danvers town archivist Richard Trask.

*The significance of the Danvers Archival Center rests with the fact that it was the first of its kind to bring together such a large collection of public and private records of a single community for purposes of preservation and accessibility to researchers. The Archives houses probably the most extensive and varied collection of materials relating to an individual municipality in New England. The collections on deposit include the local history holdings of the Danvers Historical Society, the library, numerous churches and town organizations, and official records of the Town of Danvers.*

*The Archival Center collects through gifts, purchase, and in cases where the material belongs to still-functioning corporate organizations, permanent deposit materials on paper relating to the history and development of Salem Village and Danvers, Massachusetts. Items collected include books, pamphlets, monographs, manuscripts, periodicals, maps, photographs, newspapers, audio and video tapes*[sic] *, films, broadsides, microforms, and architectural drawings.*[36]

36. Salem Witch Trials Documentary Archives and Transcription Project, Danvers Archival Center Web site (http://etext.virginia.edu/salem/witchcraft/Collection.html).

## Model 3

## Documentation in Small Steps

### Winchester Archives and Historical Society

Early collections of the Winchester Historical and Genealogical Society were housed in the Town Library and Town Hall in 1887. After changing locations several times during the twentieth century, the historical collections were secured in 1974 under the auspices of the new Winchester Archival Center, located in an historic building, the Sanborn House Carriage House. During the 1970s and '80s, the Archival Center was at its most active, with a part-time archivist leading (paid half by the town and half by the Historical Society) and volunteers assisting. It served as the prime repository for preserving Winchester's archives in an organized way; collecting documents and manuscripts, photographs, and artifacts offered by donors; and actively pursuing materials the Archives staff recognized as important to the vitality of Winchester's cultural memory. In 1989, the paid position was eliminated due to budget cuts; the records were moved to Town Hall and the artifacts placed in storage. Today, the town provides a small office with a storage vault in Town Hall, as well as a modest budget for supplies and equipment. Volunteer staff provide limited reference service and process collections.

The efforts of Winchester citizens to care for their history are a demonstration in perseverance and small successes. Serving a town population of about 20,000 residents, those interested in historic preservation established the "Collaborative for Documenting Winchester's History," which is a public/private partnership and includes representatives from the Archives, the Winchester Historical Society, the Winchester Public

Library, the town clerk's office, and the Historical Commission. The group hired me as a consultant to enhance an active archives management program upon receipt of a grant from the Massachusetts Historical Records Advisory Board (MHRAB) in 2003. The collaborative chose a database software package to catalog collections and also developed written policies and procedures for their handling. I trained volunteers to process collections and helped set goals for the future of the archives. The Winchester Historical Society is currently working to raise community awareness about historical records to enhance its community presence and to develop stronger documentation efforts.

In an age of cost-cutting, Winchester's current work aims to raise awareness about the need for collaboration when major changes and advances in an archives management program cannot be afforded. Armed with consultant recommendations and plans from an architect familiar with the needs of historical materials, the town clerk and Historical Society have set long-term sights on creating a climate-controlled, secure facility for the storage of artifacts and historical records; this facility shall maintain early public records, manuscripts, records of organizations, and photographs important to the town. A National Endowment for the Humanities (NEH) Preservation Assistance Grant allowed them to evaluate a local historic building as a possible centralized repository for historic records in Winchester. This location, known as the Sanborn House Historical and Cultural Center, has been leased to the Historical Society by the town for fifty years. One of the few remaining historic grant estates in Winchester, the house was designed in the Beaux-Arts style in 1908. The push to restore the well-known building and the drive to use the facility as a center for historical research and community events enable cultural heritage organizations to raise local awareness of historical preservation issues in a highly visible way.

Although grant money enabled the town to take the first important steps toward gaining better control of all records in Winchester without the guidance of a permanent town archivist, it is perseverance that keeps things moving forward. The collaborative recognizes the benefits of having a professional to care for materials. An additional small grant to provide training in archives management to anyone who handles historical records in Winchester has enabled the Historical Society to offer workshops in providing professional care for materials. Focusing on members of associations within the town, the training has educated the public about how to care for historical records and why it is important. It has also informed record-holders and potential donors about the work of the Archival Center and the Historical Society. These efforts enable the cultural heritage repositories to continue to make themselves visible in town so more expensive projects can immediately be resumed and an archivist perhaps be hired when finances allow.

Sometimes the road toward efficient management of records is bumpy. Without a straight line toward accomplishing the major goal, many organizations grow discouraged and give up any dream of securing a comprehensive archives management program within a secure facility. The Winchester example of a public/private collaboration demonstrates how passionate people can work toward their goals, waiting until opportunities arise to institute plans one small step at a time.

## The Cultural Heritage Partners

As discussed in Chapter One, "The Who, What, and Why of Collecting Historical Records," those who collect historical records work in many institutions and have many different backgrounds. Such diversity naturally creates challenges for collaboration. How can volunteers and professionals from different fields work together successfully? In addition to the differences between the people caring for historical records, there is great variety among our institutions and towns. How can a town with a population of 2,500 or fewer — with limited resources — be as successful in its documentation and collection development as a large city?

Within the group of those who care for our cultural heritage, there is much diversity. Cultural heritage partners can hold a Ph.D. or a high school diploma. Volunteers and professionals working in the diverse organizations we discussed earlier in this book must learn to work together. No matter their backgrounds or the makeup of their communities, it is possible for anyone to begin to apply the principles and examples in this book. Though many cultural heritage repositories do not require degreed professionals to run them, it is important for those who care for archival records and other historical resources to have a basic understanding of professional standards of care to ensure the safety of our cultural heritage. This chapter begins with a discussion about overcoming exclusionary views that hinder the care of diverse types of collections. It then discusses the professionals who care for historical records and their diverse methodologies. The chapter will then move on to the quasi-professionals who manage or work with records professionally, but who do not necessarily have a degree involving collection management. The discussion about the individuals involved with caring for archival records will be rounded out by the role of nonprofessionals, including the challenges they face and their unique perspectives that can help propel collaborative projects.

The cultural heritage repositories to which we devote our care are unique places that promote learning and self-discovery through their collections. According to author David Carr, "The great cultural institution is formative and collaborative. It assists the construction of personal knowledge in handmade lives. It tends to illuminate the unanticipated possibilities of knowing and feeling latent in one life. It inspires and extends the unpredictable reaches of personal knowledge and insight. It offers its users an array of guiding maps, lived lives, and lived experiences. These maps evolve with the learner over time; they mix design and hope with accident and wonder. They invite the learner in and lead the learner on."[37]

Such institutions are charged with collecting, preserving, and providing access to artifacts, publications, and archives that contain information with inherent community significance. Collections promote the dissemination of human ideas, bringing together individuals from diverse backgrounds for a sense of community, commonality, and partnership. "We all [as citizens] want an opportunity to feel smart and able, to feel that, even in the everyday, some bit of original wisdom is possible. We seek authenticity and integrity, solace and guidance, an idea of what other hands have constructed or other minds have made clear. Cultural institutions are the only places in our world where this can happen."[38]

---

37. David Carr, *The Promise of Cultural Institutions* (Walnut Creek, CA: AltaMira Press, 2003), 158.
38. Carr, xviii.

Professionals in the fields of archives management, library science, and museum studies possess somewhat disparate philosophies that suit the care of the particular types of materials on which their institution focuses. But in the end, we are all handling cultural resources that benefit the populace for their educational value, inherent community-building properties, recreational opportunities, and harboring of knowledge that will benefit from a broad overview of our collecting principles. Furthermore, though we may focus on either artifacts, books, or archives, our institutions tend to "dabble" in all types of material culture resources. Our inclination is to place less emphasis on the collections that we do not see as our prime focus. Sometimes, the neglect of these materials is due to lack of knowledge related to appropriate practices for their care. We need to overcome this and recognize that the diverse collections support one another.

"Archivists are professionals with the power of defining and making accessible the primary sources of history, primary sources that protect rights, educate students, inform the public, and support a primal human desire to understand our past."[39] We need to have a broad perspective of our collections — to consider the stories our institution is trying to tell and to collect resources according to how they best elucidate this story. If an institution is unprepared to deal with diverse material, it must work to rectify this through cooperation. If you choose to avoid collecting certain cultural heritage resources that relate to your organization's mission, the institution must evaluate its reason for doing so and seek partnerships with others who can better accommodate various collection items rather than maintaining improperly preserved and uncatalogued items on our shelves.

---

39. Greene, 40.

It is to the benefit of a collaborative to encourage the group to make the most of each member's expertise. We can share our skills and learn how to weave together diverse methods from the different fields. We can take advantage of the librarians' cataloging skills, the archivists' preservation skills, and the curators' interpretive skills. We can be inspired by the nonprofessionals' propensity to collect a wide variety of materials relating to a particular subject, rather than focusing primarily on the collecting of materials in a particular form. "Together, institutions that see aspects of a problem differently can constructively explore their differences."[40] By exploring our collections' strengths and weakness as a whole, we can aid in our sense of a shared purpose and shared identity.

> *One of nature's most fascinating perversities is the tendency to split into exclusive, often competing, groups. This is especially true in modern bureaucratic societies, where distinctions are often drawn on the basis of profession. Although more benign than many other sorts of clannishness, these distinctions often defy common logic and common interest. Such is the case with archivists and museum professionals. We do not read, or write for, each other's professional literature. We are unaware of all but the most public developments in each others' professions. Like other long separated groups, we have developed specialized languages and distinct methodologies, even for describing or carrying out similar functions...*[41]

---

40. Liz Bishoff, "The Collaboration Imperative," *Library Journal* (January 2004): 34.
41. John A Fleckner, "An Archivist Speaks to the Museum Profession," quoted in Kristin Parker's "The Blurred Line: A Museum Registrar Turns Archivist," New England Archivist's Newsletter (January 2009).

To make collaboration successful, we must help others understand where our methods may diverge from theirs. For example, it is not intuitive for a librarian or museum professional to consider records in groups as archivists do. They are more likely to treat each record on an item-level basis. Professionals must be prepared to explain why they do the things they do and how it can help their colleagues. A basic understanding of diverse theory is important for the professional and nonprofessional alike to ensure that everyone can apply basic principles of collection development and care developed from sound professional practice. Working from standards, we can more easily collaborate and build sound collections.

Most collaborative cultural repositories that maintain various media require the expertise of individuals from diverse yet related fields, though they may not acknowledge or recognize this. Libraries and historical societies maintaining local history collections generally wind up with at least some artifacts, archives, and monographs related to the history of their town in their collections. While naturally fitting together to form a story about the local community, these three types of materials have varying needs in terms of their preservation and organizational requirements, yet the materials often do not receive differing care due to lack of knowledge, emphasis on a particular type of material, or insufficient resources for proper storage and application of appropriate procedures. A collaborative can help overcome these problems by providing a support system for the care of diverse items.

The collaborative group should aim to offer training for all collaborative members to acquaint them with diverse practices. Such training can build a sense of community among cultural caretakers and shows commonalities between uncommon professions. Non-archivists can learn to relate archival procedures to their own training, and archivists can learn procedures from other cultural heritage professionals that they can adapt to diverse collections. Explaining the differences between materials will make collaborators more amenable to each other's methods and help them develop mutual respect.

Much recent literature has focused on "LAM." This acronym brings together the broad worlds of libraries, archives, and museums.[42] The literature reflects the need to more greatly explore the relationships between the three related professions. The work of Margaret Hedstrom and John Leslie King focusing on the LAM invites us to find "commonalities of collecting" and to examine how our collections, and our different ways of working with them, benefit society. The authors see a broad responsibility for cultural heritage collections to provide resources for the naturally curious mind to inquire and seek answers to questions about culture and humanity. "The selection processes that professional librarians, archivists, and curators carry out are essential filtering mechanisms based on professional norms and standards, subject, and domain knowledge, and attentiveness to the needs of user communities.... An essential function of the LAM is the accumulation and preservation of knowledge that might someday be of vital importance. Libraries, archives, and museums maintain collections over the course of centuries. The LAM are the most important form of long-term social memory."[43]

The future success of the LAM relies on how well we work together to create collections that are meaningful to the public. This success also rests upon our aptitude to articulate our commonalities and to explain the value of all cultural heritage collections. Those writing about the LAM

---

42. Margaret Hedstrom and John Leslie King, "Epistemic Infrastructure in the Rise of the Knowledge Economy," *Advancing Knowledge and the Knowledge Economy*, eds. Brian Kahin and Dominque Foray (Cambridge, MA: MIT Press, 2007), 113–34.
43. Hedstrom and King, conclusion.

see a cross-professional responsibility to promote the value of the materials within all of our repositories, encouraging professionals to appreciate materials in formats differing from the ones in which they specialize and to recognize how our materials support each other. "LAM professionals who understand issues surrounding different types of collections and collecting institutions, and who are not rigidly wedded to their own professional traditions, bring an open-mindedness that allows them to embrace ideas from other professions in the interest of collaboration."[44]

The work of librarians, archivists, and curators can reach different audiences with crossed purposes to promote knowledge, modernization, and change. Collectively, the idea of the LAM provides a great opportunity to demonstrate the importance of cultural heritage resources to a larger audience than archives, libraries, and museums can individually. Outreach opportunities that explain the value of cultural collections are seen on a small scale by the curator, who creates an exhibit to which a young child enthusiastically responds, or by the librarian, who opens a book to reveal information a patron could not find on the Internet. Similarly, the archivist who recognizes a missing piece of history in a document that remained in an attic for twenty years and the volunteer who shares an innate love of his work with his neighbor have the capacity and responsibility to build sound collections, using their expertise to relate the tangible and intangible values of cultural resources to the public.[45] Working together, the opportunities to share materials and our experience can reach way beyond what any one field can reach alone.

---

44. Diane M Zorich, Gunter Waibel, and Ricky Erway, 27.
45. Gerald Beasley's "Curatorial Crossover: Building Library, Archives and Museum Collections" describes the blurring of libraries, archives, and museums and the goal of culture heritage collaborators to reflect the tangible and intangible wonders of their collections.

People and organizations with diverse backgrounds can work together using their varied knowledge and resources to form effective partnerships for the maintenance of archival records. Partners can use their expertise to communicate the vision of a collaborative and its benefits to a community. There is more than one way to accomplish communal goals for collection development and to establish working relationships. Partnerships are most successful when diversity and distinct identities are appreciated. Collaborative entities should represent a community's cultural values and be founded on the diversified expertise of cultural heritage partners.

## *The Professional Cultural Heritage Collaborators*

The professionals who care for cultural heritage resources include individuals educated in library science, museum studies, and archives management. The following paragraphs describe the fields and the types of collections on which each professional focuses. Included is a short discussion about the role each professional should play in a collaborative.

Library science primarily involves the care of secondary sources, including books, periodicals, mass-produced recordings, and computerized information. Secondary-source materials include nonoriginal sources of information that are often published and distributed en masse. Librarians sort and catalog information. They often rely on descriptions already provided by other institutions for the same materials. Libraries (except in the case of rare-book collections) focus more on the importance of the information contained within the materials than on the materials themselves.

The role of the nonspecialist or public librarian among their cultural heritage peers is to assist with research-based inquiry and to help others make informed decisions about secondary resources that can support the cultural heritage repository. Librarian expertise in the area of classification and technology can greatly assist with the development of culturally based projects. Librarians also excel at making information accessible and available to the public. The librarian can work to compile secondary-source materials that support the unique collections of their peers in the cultural heritage professions. This will help form a complete view of a documented subject. The special librarian with subject specialization can supplement available heritage knowledge related to a particular theme through their collection development practices. Within a collaborative, a subject specialist can help boost available supplementary information related to particular issues, as well as provide guidance in community documentation strategies related to these topics.

Libraries were once the cornerstone of intellectual and moral development. As institutions, public libraries stood as vanguards of all facets of civilization's activities. In the mid-nineteenth century, public libraries were established to promote culture, refinement, and education. Many libraries aimed to disseminate knowledge to "pull up" the middle and working classes. Toward this end, libraries promoted the arts, science, and literature through all their endeavors. The institutions began designing programs to aid lifelong education and to put together collections that assisted their end goals. Working men's libraries (mechanics' institutes) provided lectures, discussions, and exhibits to feed into the public's fascination with diverse "things" that helped define and reflect society.[46] These "things" included books, artifacts,

---

46. The diversity of activities launched by nineteenth-century libraries is discussed in D.W. Davies in *Public Libraries as Culture and Social Centers: The Origin of the Concept* (Metuchen, NJ: The Scarecrow Press Inc., 1974). Though Davies promotes his

and other items that had the ability to challenge and expand an individual's knowledge about himself and the world around him. Buildings were erected as monuments to house collections, and communities came to value these edifices and see them as symbolic representations of their pride. Crossing over into the activities we now define as reserved for museum professionals and archivists, librarians had, and still have, the capacity to pull together communities with these resources under the umbrella of "culture."

Museology (or "museum studies") involves the care of artifacts. Though generally unique sources, these materials are designed using various media, for which diverse preservation techniques are required. The artifact itself is as important as the information that can be elicited from it. Museum objects are cataloged and organized individually, relying on information about an object's creator, medium, dates, subject, and distinguishing features.[47] Special care is taken to preserve the original item, and special emphasis is often given for its protection, which usually takes precedence over its accessibility.

The role of the museum professional is to interpret culturally valuable material, to fit it into a cultural context and make the ideas the object invokes understandable to the general public. Among his cultural heritage peers, the museum professional is generally best at reaching out to the public and at making history fun and valid for modern life through exhibits and programming. For collaborative collection development purposes, the museum specialist may assist other experts with their work in interpretation and understanding the broader context of materials, while

---

belief in the value of librarians primarily to support reading, the past twenty years have shown the value of the librarian's generalist role in gathering and disseminating information in diverse formats. As generalists, librarians have a valuable role to play in collection development and in promoting the community collaboration.

47. See the International Council of Museums Object ID checklist for standards on cataloging in museums at http://icom.museum/object-id/checklist.html.

spreading their vital outreach work to benefit collaboration in general.

Museums evolved alongside libraries. Early "museum" collections were established by private collectors. In the mid-nineteenth century, governments began to provide libraries and museums with tax support. Libraries and museums were often housed in the same buildings established by public philanthropists, who provided initial support in exchange for community government assurance of future funding. Locals established institutions such as the Boston Athenaeum to serve as cultural centers that housed reading materials and artifacts. These cultural institutions were intended to uplift society, providing resources for entertainment and scholarship. Soon the museum evolved and pulled away from the library, defining its separate purpose and establishing its own methodologies. Today, the museum professional works to preserve and interpret the unique artifacts of man that elucidate the development of civilization, providing the community with resources to reexamine itself and its cultural mores.

Archives management involves the care of unique original documents and other multi-formats of historical records. When used in research, archival materials are usually closest to the event or activity they describe and are therefore more reliable than, but most useful when used in tandem with, secondary materials for studying history. Archival materials include: diaries, letters, account books, manuscripts, original sound and video recordings, photographs, and digital media. Like museum objects, archives are cataloged based on the material at hand. Because of their unique nature, archives cannot rely on descriptions provided by other institutions with similar sources. Unlike artifacts or books, archives are generally organized in groupings of materials, with less importance placed on an individual item and more emphasis placed on a set of documents or a "collection." Special care is taken to preserve the original item whenever possible, but if the item cannot be saved, an archivist will take pains to preserve the information contained within the source.

The role of the archivist is to preserve, describe, and provide access to historical records within a particular collecting focus. Archivists must use their skills to assist with the development of a documentary record that boosts research and historical understanding across cultural repositories. Within a collaborative, an archivist should help a community recognize the value of its historical records. The archivist must make others aware of the pervasiveness of records in our society. With skills in appraisal, the archivist can play a guiding role to help others use their own expertise to make appropriate collection development decisions. Archivists act as "mediators between record creators and records repositories, archives and users, between conceptions of the past and extant documents."[48]

Records have been saved by civilizations to refer to for conventional (financial and legal) purposes, to promote cultures, and (in democratized societies) to ensure protection against government abuses. Archives were given special treatment for centuries as symbols of an individual society's advancement. In the eighteenth century, "Nations began to centralize and consolidate their records and erect special buildings as proof of their country's importance and commitment to history."[49] Archives were first retained in government centers, then later in institutions of higher learning. In the United States, local and regional centers flourished in the nineteenth century due to a growth in

48. Francis X. Blouin, "Archivists, Mediation, and the Constructs of Social Memory," *Archival Issues* 24. 2 (1999): 111.

49. Ed. James Gregory Bradsher, *Managing Archives and Archival Institutions* (Chicago: University of Chicago Press, 1988): 24.

record creation, newborn patriotism that citizens wanted reflected in their cultural resources, and a belief in democracy that relied on the preservation and facilitation of access to government records.[50] Methods of care during this time first focused on the needs of scholars, arranging records by area of popular study based on methods of librarianship. Archives management then turned toward reflecting the environment in which the records were created. The development of distinct methods of archives management mimicked new ideology that placed value on cultural knowledge. Archivists today work to reflect all aspects of diverse societies by collecting the records of various groups and individuals.

Today, the seemingly disparate fields of library science, museum studies, and archives management harbor professionals who work in a wide variety of institutions with various missions and institutional cultures. Some may be surrounded by related professionals in a university setting or a large town or city; others may be lone professionals within a small town. Whatever their circumstances, these professionals can help propel a collaborative using their expertise and a shared sense of history. Bound by a dedication to promoting and reflecting culture and diverse societies, born of shared tradition, cultural heritage institutions must work together using the manmade resources in their repositories to advance the care of their collections.[51]

---

50. Randall C. Jimerson provides a detailed discussion of the rise of the archives profession and its relationship to democratic ideals in his book *Archives Power: Memory, Accountability, and Social Justice* (Chicago: Society of American Archivists, 2009), Chapter 2.

51. Museums, libraries, and archives emerged from the Renaissance and blossomed during the Enlightenment. Promoting the growth of knowledge, men began collections to "elicit wonder" and then to encourage "inquiring and theorizing." For a comprehensive look at the development of cultural heritage organizations, see Hedstrom and King.

### *The Quasi-Professional Cultural Heritage Collaborators*

Quasi-professionals include those who care for or about historical records and/or cultural artifacts as part of their duties, but who do not focus exclusively on the maintenance, preservation, and use of these materials for cultural purposes. These individuals also may or may not have formal training in the management of such materials. Town clerks and researchers are the two largest caretakers falling into this category.

Town or city clerks are legally charged with the responsibility to preserve, maintain, and provide access to the public records in their municipalities. The records in their possession which hold permanent value are generally governed by statute and include the following:

- Proprietary records — telling us about the establishment of local government
- Vital records — telling us about individual citizens' births, marriages, and deaths
- Meeting minutes — describing the functioning of town government
- Assessments — describing property and property values
- Bylaws and charters — providing information about town government operations and ensuring the continual operation of the town
- Plans, maps, and deeds — providing information about town land growth, use, and development
- Account books — telling us about town spending and interests
- School and church records — usually the earliest local "government" records (pre–American Revolution, when lines between religion and government were blurred) telling us about social, spiritual, and educational development

Clerks are required to secure archival records in their possession through appropriate preservation practices, including the use of archival enclosures for the housing of records and the maintenance of secure environments. As the Freedom of Information Act and similar statutes require that the citizenry has access to the public records created by their government, clerks must ensure that records are accessible. Larger collections and those maintained by the most organized of clerks are often cataloged. Some municipalities have developed digital systems for the maintenance and sharing of information. Since the clerk is charged with caring for such valuable cultural heritage resources, it is imperative to include them on the list of cultural collaborators. Clerks have varying levels of expertise. Those in small towns may work part-time and have limited exposure to historical records. Those in large towns or cities may have greater responsibilities and knowledge in areas related to the care and development of their own collections.

It is common to find municipal records in repositories outside of a clerk's jurisdiction or in the hands of private individuals, even though this is prohibited by law. Records were sometimes taken by government employees for safekeeping or out of a desire to retain materials they created in their day-to-day activities. Some government archives are also scattered due to neglect or mismanagement. Collaborative work can do much to help return government records to clerks and their Archives and make individuals aware of the importance of keeping public information available and centralized.

Researchers are another quasi-professional group and are strongly tied to the interests of cultural heritage resources. The materials in the possession of cultural heritage repositories are what they use to develop their own theories and to write books. Researchers include professors from universities and colleges, upper-level students, independent authors writing nonfiction or historically based fiction, and genealogists. These individuals work with cultural resources regularly and must familiarize themselves with a wide variety of heritage-based materials and the methods professionals employ for their care.

I recently attended a conference for archivists where an author made a presentation about the value of archivists and librarians. In her presentation, she praised the professionals for helping her find records related to her biographical research about an eighteenth-century African-American woman.[52] She also noted that, through her research, she and her husband found many records in private hands and tried to convince individuals to place valuable documents in appropriate repositories. Her husband located one large series of early American records vital to their research in the attic of a Vermont courthouse; the series had been picked at by vermin. The author made efforts to make authorities aware of the value of the records, and work is now being done to save the materials and house them appropriately. This demonstrates that the diverse subject knowledge, knowledge of resources, and passion of the researcher can help propel any collaborative collection development efforts.

Records managers are also members of the quasi-professional cultural heritage collaborators group. Though charged with the professional management of records, which in many cases also have significance as archives, most records managers in the United States do not concern themselves with the cultural value of the materials in their possession. Records managers maintain records when they are needed for administrative purposes. They care for

---

52. Gretchen Holbrook Gerzina's presentation at the Spring 2009 New England Archivists Conference on her book, *Mr. and Mrs. Prince: How an Extraordinary Eighteenth-Century Family Moved Out of Slavery and Into Legend* (New York, NY: Amistad Press, 2008).

institutional records that are regularly used by an organization's staff (but not on a daily basis). Records managers concern themselves with legal compliance and the transfer of records to less expensive storage space or disposition. Records managers often work with archivists to ensure records with perpetual value are retained indefinitely and transferred to archival storage. (In some cases, a records manager is also a professional archivist or is charged with an archivist's duties.)

### *The Nonprofessional Cultural Heritage Collaborators*

Nonprofessionals who create or maintain cultural resources include those who do not fall into the professional or quasi-professional categories. They may have an interest in seeing records preserved or may have awareness of the historical value of the materials they maintain. They may be eager to play a role in preserving culture or less willing to participate in a collaborative process.

First, nonprofessionals include the volunteers who run many of the small historical societies and museums across the country. They bring a sense of excitement to the work that they do, generally working purely for the love of history or their community. The expertise of nonprofessionals in handling collections varies greatly. Some recognize the need for applying standards and work hard to incorporate a professional ethic in what they do. Others have their own ideas about the best ways to handle collections, acquiring and organizing based on gut feeling rather than on theory or generally accepted practice. Volunteers often also become the "town historians" and may have a deeper knowledge about a broad spectrum of their community history than anyone else in town.

The role of volunteers is to ensure that the history of their community is saved. When no one else steps forward to care for a community's history, or no money is perceived as available for developing cultural heritage collecting programs, the responsibility falls to a volunteer in many small towns (and even, sometimes, in larger ones). Volunteers bring an overall perspective to a collaborative, reminding us that it is the documentation and preservation of our history and sense of culture that is important, sometimes helping the professional shed an obsession with the material-based resources alone. Nonprofessionals can be aided by professionals within a collaborative (when professionals are available for inclusion) through the teaching of standards and how to apply techniques toward the care of materials. The professional would also do well to listen to the volunteers' diverse viewpoints.

Second, businesses within a town possess an important piece of the American documentary record. The records that are created daily by businessmen and American workers provide important information about the functioning of our society. Businesses that work to preserve their own records should be aware of the importance of their material resources beyond their individual institutions. Many businesses manage their own records through records-management programs and retention schedules. A great many more have no formal plans in place for the care of these materials. Businesses may share information about their histories with repositories. Defunct businesses may wish to deposit their unique records of permanent value with appropriate repositories to ensure that their place in society is remembered. According to archivist Adrian Cunningham:

> *By raising awareness of the importance of records, record collectors can also help record creators better track their materials to assist them during*

> *their active lives. Archivists and others familiar with cataloging, indexing, and organizational techniques can teach others how to employ them so that recordkeeping is more efficient and access to information is easier. Teaching record creators how to properly organize and describe information will also allow them to send records to our archives in a more useful way, so that they are fully documented and ready for accession. This cuts down on the time we need to take to arrange, interpret, and otherwise process materials.*
>
> *... collecting archives in the next millennium will need to collaborate more closely with record creators, they will need to actively promote the value of good recordkeeping practices to those who operate in unregulated or semi-regulated recordkeeping environments and they will need to work towards the embedding of desirable recordkeeping attributes in the design of software programs used by such record keepers... I believe that we need to acquire a better understanding of recordkeeping in unregulated environments... We need to acquire a better understanding of the dynamics of personal recordkeeping behavior* [53]

Beyond the records themselves, businessmen can play a leading role in propelling collaborative efforts through their political clout and with monetary resources often available to nonprofits. Corporations and small businesses looking to establish a community presence do well to work collaboratively with culturally based

---

53. Adrian Cunningham, *Collecting Archives in the Next Millennium* (paper presented to the Australian Society of Archives; July 1997). Available online at www.nla.gov.au/nla/staffpaper/acunning7.html.

organizations. Businesses can serve as sponsors of special projects. These public/private partnerships are regaining momentum as individuals from nonprofits, local governments, and businesses realize the advantages of partnering for community revitalization and economic development. When these three sectors collaborate, everyone can benefit from increased promotion, outreach, and tangible results made possible by combining knowledge and resources.[54]

Third, representatives from local churches and civic associations also make valuable partners in a collaborative. These organizations generally create records that are vital to the understanding of community life. It is important to help them understand the importance of their records so that the materials may be properly maintained. Like businesses, civic entities bring a unique perspective to a partnership, and they often have their own specialized collections to consider. Their continually growing institutional archives can generally be most efficiently managed in-house to ensure that new records are continually reviewed for their historical value. A collaborative encourages more institutions like these to preserve their own cultural heritage resources toward the "greater good," which helps with the efficient documentation and preservation of various aspects of a community. Within a partnership, individuals who participate in civic organizations can provide a wealth of knowledge about their communities to a collaborative. They often also become ardent supporters of cultural

---

54. See Christopher T. Gates, "Forum: Democracy and the Civic Museum," *Museum News (*May/June 2001) for an examination of the challenges of public/private partnerships. In the 1970s, this kind of partnering was a very popular way for nonprofits to try to solve some of the problems they encountered. However, concerns often arise when businesses are given too much reign. As with any collaborator, a corporate partner must be treated with respect and must be prepared to treat his cultural heritage partners the same way.

heritage institutions through volunteerism and public endorsement of preservation efforts and other activities. .

Finally, the records of individuals must not be forgotten. Personal papers, often left undiscovered in private homes, tell what it was like to live in a particular place at a particular time. Within cultural heritage institutions around the United States are the papers of citizens that shed light on life in a particular community at a particular time. It is important for repositories to see the individuals within their communities as nonprofessional partners who likely possess important pieces of historical documentation. Institutions collecting records can help make them aware of the value of their materials, may encourage them to take part in a dialogue about history, and may gently prod them to properly preserve and perhaps provide access to the resources they maintain

## Model 4

## Volunteers Handling Public Records:

### Gloucester Archives

The City of Gloucester, located on Cape Ann, Massachusetts, was America's first working seaport and was formally incorporated in 1642. In 1873, the town was reincorporated as a city and now has a population of about 30,000 people. The City Archives document the almost 375-year history of the community, through official government records that are maintained under the supervision of the city clerk by local volunteers.

According to state government statutes, municipal clerks are responsible for the maintenance of public records as outlined by formal record-retention schedules. Local governments must maintain archival material in appropriate storage vaults and facilitate access to the information within the materials.

Within Massachusetts, municipal clerks maintain legal custody of public records; therefore, record programs designed for the safekeeping of public records fall under their management. Because a clerk has numerous and diverse duties, records management often does not get the attention it needs and that is required by law. Gloucester, Massachusetts, has used volunteers for more than two decades to assist the clerk with maintaining and providing appropriate access to materials. Their work has encouraged the city to properly care for its historical records, and their efforts have harnessed support from the city government to try to set up a formal public-records management program.

In the late 1980s, a resident with an interest in rare books helped form an archives committee in Gloucester. The group's creation was prompted by a concern with the conditions of the vaults in Gloucester's City Hall. Though most of the original committee soon disbanded, other volunteers joined and received training in the care of archival records from Massachusetts' Archives. At first, the volunteers worked in hallways to review the materials held in fourteen government vaults. They then went into offices to review records, sought grants for preservation, created plans for the future of the archives, and established an office in the basement of the building.

Over time, assistants came and went. Today, two volunteers who joined the original stalwarts run the Gloucester Archives with the help of five additional active volunteers, including the archivist from the local Cape Ann Museum. The group still works in a small, cramped office space and is still retrieving records from the same old vaults, but the conditions for access are much improved. Many records have been conserved; all records are retained in acid-free boxes. Most importantly, the volunteers have raised awareness about the need to care for archival resources. Based on their work, the city even passed an ordinance to establish an archives and records advisory commission and opened the door for the possibility of one day employing a professional archivist and creating a more advanced facility for the storage of records.

The volunteers primarily spend their days answering questions using the records in their care. This gives them a lot of visibility and a good reputation. The Archives is able to provide the mayor and other municipal departments with any information they need. This visibility has translated into an ability to raise money for necessary items through donations. And, although things are moving slowly, decisions are being made about the future of City Hall involving modeling or rebuilding. The best means to care for the archives will be taken into account when construction plans are finalized.

Without a lot of money or even permanent staff, Gloucester has done much to ensure the longevity of its public community records. Dedicated citizens play an important role in preserving some of the most important documents in their city. Consistency in leadership of volunteers who train each other and make use of available grant programs has enabled them to keep their work active. No matter what the conditions and circumstances of local records, much can be done to ensure their care with perseverance and commitment. Archivists strive for an ideal that may not be easily attainable; they should not be discouraged by setbacks.

**Summary of Cultural Heritage Collaborators**

| Professionals | Quasi-Professionals | Nonprofessionals |
|---|---|---|
| Archivists | Town clerks | Volunteers |
| Librarians | Researchers | Businessmen |
| Curators | Records managers | Office administrators |
| | | Association secretaries |
| | | Individuals |

Archivists, librarians, and curators who handle historical collections can guide others and focus on the need to properly manage and develop the historical record.

Town clerks and record managers who handle records on a day-to-day basis can recognize a need to build rich collections of archives that provide cultural information and serve as evidence of the functioning of society. They can work to ensure that appropriate papers under their jurisdiction end up in appropriate permanent housing where they are preserved and accessible to the public.

Researchers who view primary-resource material regularly can assist with building a rich documentary record by supporting cultural heritage institutions and their endeavors through research, identification of missing information, and sometimes location of that information. Researchers have the capacity to serve as intermediaries between private record-holders and professionals within repositories. They can also be advocates for cultural heritage institutions, encouraging a public interested in their work to value archives.

Volunteers can lend their support to cultural heritage institutions through their unpaid assistance. They are also advocates in the community, raising recognition of the value of archival programs by vocalizing their support among their neighbors.

Like town clerks and record managers, the businessmen, office administrators, and association secretaries who create the records of organizations can make efforts to see a bigger picture of how these records have historical import. They can work with professionals to see if their documents add value to a community archive.

Individuals can also be encouraged to see the value of their personal papers beyond themselves and their families. They can choose to contribute appropriate documents to a professional repository to enhance the documentary record.

All collaborators can bring personal expertise to the discussion of community documentation and help identify what materials should be part of the effort to form a complete documentary record.

---

## Donor Relations

Donors are a very important part of the cultural heritage collaborative partnership. People working in repositories who develop positive relationships within their communities will find more opportunities for collection development. Private citizens often possess exciting materials that can help fill gaps in the documentary record. Within the category of nonprofessional cultural heritage collaborators are those individuals who may create personal records in their homes, as well as those who may involve themselves with other aspects of their communities (businesses and associations) that generate archives. This section provides information about how to work with this unique group — one that is often forgotten when pursuing collaborative projects. Every person with whom we come into contact is a potential donor who may possess important records that fill gaps in the historic record and tell something about the society in which we live. Cultural heritage institutions must keep this in mind and work to make our public aware of the role they have to play in what we do.

Important community records are those that give us a flavor for the history and culture of a town, including its citizens, jobs, recreational activities, events, and development. Archivists who actively reach out to members of their communities can find "lost" public documents in private homes and other notable archives worthy of placement in collecting repositories. Record caretakers must help the community recognize the value of the records that they create in their personal and professional lives by explaining how these records reflect society.

To raise awareness about the significance of an individual's personal papers to a larger community, a cultural heritage professional must prepare to describe his collecting purpose in layman's terms to individuals or groups of patrons. Archivists must get better at explaining the role of their collections to nonprofessionals. Where the function of a museum or library collection is obvious to most (though not always properly appreciated), the role of an archives facility is often more puzzling to outsiders.

The stories of all of the individuals and families within a neighborhood form a picture of an American community — our differing beliefs, functions, family structures — that reflect the whole of our society. These stories are useful for all kinds of researchers who want to discover more about our past and about their heritage. What we know about history is based on the documentary record, the surviving written or otherwise recorded information. Records residing in private residences might change our perspective about history. Records protected by repositories aim to give us a balanced view, demonstrating multiple aspects of society and multiple viewpoints. Personal papers lost to time or remaining in private hands, undiscovered by historians, could have the potential to change our perceptions of our culture and ourselves.

In addition to the records found in private homes, the written materials created by local associations and businesses tell us much about everyday life and the makeup of a community. While large businesses generally have their own records management and archives programs that ensure the longevity of their history, many small businesses come and go, with their records lost to time. Local shops, small companies, and even sole proprietorships form part of the American story. The records of their formation and activities are of value to local history. Similarly, organizations such as Rotaries, garden clubs, mothers' groups, and others that exist to enhance the lives of citizens have archival materials of value for community documentation. In fact, the long existence of many of these groups in locales ties them strongly to and reveals much about community roots and culture.

Institutions must use outreach opportunities to explain how the records created during the course of day-to-day activities tell the story of what it is or was like to live during a particular time. Showing off a repository's personal papers, to which audiences can relate, greatly impacts views about the role of archives in documenting community heritage. Diaries, account books, photographs, and other recognizable items from the collections can help potential donors make connections between their family records and the Archives. It is necessary to demonstrate how personal materials make up vital portions of American repositories. It is important to relate that such documents retained by repositories do not necessarily come from well-known individuals. Special collections are built on the common stories of American citizens with diverse backgrounds.

The types of materials Archives collect and why people may want to use them should be explained through these public outreach efforts. Exhibits can show off personal papers from the collection. Programming can provide even greater opportunities for interaction with potential community collaborators, presenting an opportunity to get valuable information of all sorts about collections' care into the community. People are appreciative of assistance that helps them create family memories and preserve them. Cultural heritage professionals can design workshops that promote creating documentation, organizing it, and preserving it. Encourage audiences to bring in their personal memorabilia and papers and use them as samples for discussing appropriate care.

Repositories should also create collection guides and brochures that show the breadth of collections and describe the value of personal papers to the repository. Look for opportunities to interject information about collections in everyday conversations across the community. Write letters to the editor of the local paper when appropriate that use samples from the archives. Create a newsletter and a column for the local paper that includes samples from the collections. Ask residents questions that get them into a dialogue about history. Simple efforts, such as publishing photographs from the collections and asking people to help name unidentified individuals in the image, have done much to raise public awareness about collections for many institutions.

Once an Archives proves the long-term value of a collection of personal papers beyond the donor and his immediate relations, the patron has a mindset that will consider the records beyond their active lives, making them more important as documents of social activity and not just papers to be used and disposed. Archivists who take the time to educate the public will find that record creators can be convinced more easily to care for their records in a way that will accommodate their permanent storage at the end of their active lives. Cultural caretakers well-versed in archives management can help with care of records within organizations and individual homes if called upon to do so. They may take the opportunity to teach about proper filing and storing materials in appropriate acid-free materials so they are kept safe for posterity. "Where private owners are aware of the importance and value of their archives, they often lack the expertise and resources necessary both to arrange and preserve their archives and to make them available for public consultation. Advice and assistance should be much more forthcoming [from archivists] than they appear to be at present…."[55]

---

55. Rosemary Seton, *The Preservation and Administration of Private Archives: A RAMP Study* (Paris: General Information Program and UNISIST, 1984), 34.

**Types of Community Records Held by Potential Donors**

Not all records can or should be saved for posterity, but the following is a list of some of the more common materials that are valuable to archival institutions and created as part of individuals' everyday activities. Ask potential donors to consider donating such materials to their local Archives or historical society to preserve the information that makes up our cultural heritage and demonstrates our intellectual and social development. Remember to seek material in a variety of formats — printed, video, audio, digital.

**Business Records**
Meeting minutes, memos and correspondence, financial records, product guides and marketing material, outreach materials and publications, planning documents, annual reports

**Personal Records**
Diaries, photographs and albums (labeled with names of people or places shown), family scrapbooks, budgets, account books, genealogies, correspondence, receipts, school papers and exams, scrapbooks, house histories, oral histories, family videos

**Association Records** (including organizations such as women's clubs, local book clubs, etc.)
Meeting minutes, memos and correspondence, financial records, event records, planning documents, bylaws and nonprofit records, membership lists, annual reports, memorabilia

While many donors at first do not recognize the value of their materials to the greater society, others are hesitant to make their personal, business, and association papers public. Records may be donated during the life of an individual or organization. Or, records may be bequeathed for transfer to an Archives after an individual's death or in the event an organization goes out of business or otherwise requires the permanent preservation of its archives. Continual outreach that makes the community aware of the value of its records will encourage people to think of archival repositories when considering the disposition of various papers. Creating a donor mentality within the community will help potential donors think of cultural repositories before a dire moment in the care and continuance of a portion of the documentary record is reached. Rather than scavenging items from the trash or exploring abandoned properties to see what materials may be suitable there for our repositories, it is possible for us to raise awareness in the community and target a record for accession into a collection before the records' useful life had ended. [56]

Some collectors may be happy to tell you about their collections but may not want to part with them or open them fully up to public scrutiny. Inviting record creators to participate in a collaborative or reaching them through outreach programs that discuss the future of local history will help educate about the reasons one may want to give private materials to an Archives. Treating a potential donor as a documenter will encourage an individual to evaluate his role in community documentation. Being made part of the process often helps individuals become more

---

56. The Society of American Archivists provides "A Guide to Donating Your Personal or Family Papers to a Repository," which can be handed out to potential donors as an outreach tool. It provides information about repositories and preservation and gives donation guidelines. See http://www.archivists.org/publications/donating-familyrecs.asp.

comfortable with discussing their personal items. Many choose to donate materials when they are convinced of their value to a larger community. Others who are unwilling to part with materials for sentimental or personal reasons may be willing to allow a repository to make microfilm or photocopies for research and preservation purposes. Some owners may be willing to have researchers referred to them if they are unwilling to part with the originals. At the very least, outreach to record creators opens lines of communication and enables archivists to speak about the value of records and personal papers. It also allows archivists to identify important resources within the community and help ensure their protection through education about methods for their care.

Repositories can alleviate concerns of potential donors about how their records will be used by a repository by addressing fears about disseminating personal information. If necessary, Archives may work with a donor to identify sensitive information that is appropriate for restriction. They may agree to prevent access to certain parts of the collection for an agreed-upon period. Though restricted access is generally undesirable to institutions, it is reasonable for families to donate materials and ask for some parts of it to be restricted until individuals who may be compromised by certain information are deceased. Institutions must consider if material encumbered by conditions imposed by the donor add a burden of time and expense that is not outweighed by the benefit of the materials' research value.

Another way repositories try to alleviate concerns of hesitant donors is by offering agreements for permanent loans. Such arrangements allow donors to keep materials preserved in a repository without signing over their physical ownership and copyrights. Permanent loans are undesirable for the institution receiving the collection because it gives the housing institution all the responsibility for caring for the materials without any of the benefits of ownership. However, many institutions do choose to take part in this kind of arrangement; a close collaborative relationship between organizations or between a private donor and a repository can help make the agreement successful. A highly desirable collection may be placed on permanent loan in a facility when donation is not possible, so the repository can fill a gap in its collection and provide a useful service to its researchers. When entering such an arrangement, a repository should require monetary assistance to preserve and care for the collection in case the donor seeks the collection's return. Repositories should try to make agreements to receive permanent ownership of the collection at a particular date.

Encouraging goodwill toward an organization beyond the donor relationship will also encourage active donating. Institutions must help the public (i.e., potential donors) see the value of their mission. They must encourage individuals to support organizations by creating an understanding of the purpose and preservation needs of the materials in collections. Community members may offer support through fundraising and volunteerism that highlights the activities of the repository while vouching for the significance of its mission. Organizations must create vibrant programs and educational opportunities that attract attention. They must make information about collections, including collection development policies, openly accessible to the public. Published collection descriptions, policies on Web pages, and copies placed in the reading rooms inform and invite potential donors. Your goal with donor relations is to make the public aware of institutional missions and development strategies to garner support needed to aid collecting goals.

Donor relations are best cultivated cooperatively. When offered a collection that is better suited for a sister repository, an institution should steer that donor to the other institution. This can be done gently, explaining why the collection is better suited for the other repository and how it will get more attention and use if it is donated to the appropriate place. Collection caretakers must not turn a donor away without suggesting alternative Archives for his donation. Referral is made easier through the creation of appropriate networked access tools that allow users to see who owns what materials in the community and within a collaborative. Comprehensive collection development policies with references to collaborative collecting institutions and institutions outside of the community with related collections can help steer donors to the locations where their materials can be best cared for and will be most used. Institutions with written collection development policies are also more likely to receive referrals of appropriate materials to their own collections, as outside institutions will better understand their focus.[57] In other words, your willingness to refer donors elsewhere will be reciprocated by other cooperative repositories, reducing competition and making for stronger collections.

It is not to the benefit of the Archives or history professions for an institution to accept a collection because of competitiveness, desire for monetary gain, or publicity. "Accepting inappropriate items will not increase a museum's stature in the community. It will only perpetuate its reputation as a repository for everything unwanted in an attic or cellar. Such a museum wastes time and money on the care of artifacts which are outside its collection scope, sacrifices valuable storage space for redundant objects, and feels obligated to exhibit unrelated artifacts in a show."[58] If

---

57. Cynthia K. Sauer discusses the benefits of using collection development policies in "Doing the Best We Can? The Use of Collection Development Policies and Cooperative Collecting Activities at Manuscript Repositories," *The American Archivist* 64.2 (Fall/Winter 2001): 327.
58. MJ Davis, "Just Say No! Nicely," Bay State Historical League, *CommonWealth* (Winter 1996–97): 2.

a collection clearly falls outside the realm of an institution's focus, it must be referred elsewhere. This is an ethical issue with which all archivists must struggle. If your institution is in need of monetary support, and a donor who can and is willing to provide additional support offers a collection, it would be extremely difficult to turn the donor away. Similarly, it can be difficult to turn away a donor who insists that his collection belongs at your repository. It is important for an archivist to gauge a donor's reaction when deciding to propose that a collection belongs at another repository. The archivist must balance his institution's needs with those of the profession and researchers, as well as the desires of a potential donor.

Politics influence an Archive's decisions when a parent organization insists that the archivist accept a collection to appease a donor, especially when the archivist knows that the collection more appropriately would be housed elsewhere. This can be especially true at places that actively pursue monetary donations from wealthy patrons for other aspects of their work when these patrons also wish to house their personal records in the Archives. As an archivist, you must make your stance on this matter known before encountering this situation. Cultural caretakers must make sure that one's administration is very familiar with the institution's collection development policy. Archivists should ask the director, a trustee, or another administrative member to sit in on collection development meetings or participate on a collections committee. Archivists must provide administrators with copies of collection development policies and set up a subsequent meeting to discuss what the policy means for the institution. Handing out a document without some kind of follow-up will almost ensure that it will not be remembered, even if it's read. Archivists must continually communicate goals with administration, making their presence within the institution known by participating on committees and by performing extensive outreach work. Archivists who make people interested in what they do and make them want to hear about progress in collection development can eradicate misconceptions about their role and interests. You must break the common stereotypes of Archives handling "any old stuff" through outreach efforts, before support is needed on important issues.

The key to donor relations is to identify appropriate potential donors, view them as partners, treat them with respect, and work with them to identify and care for records with long-term value. Cultural heritage collaborators must not wait for donors to come to them. Filling gaps in the documentary record involves detective work. You must use your network of collaborators to determine who in the community might have valuable materials related to a specific collecting focus. Looking beyond the big names alone and promoting a documentation project to the general community can save documents with valuable information that describe everyday life. Involving record creators in the collection development process when their records are first written and as they are used helps the creator to actively prepare his records for possible donation to your institution. Offering services to help identify and preserve older historical records in private custodianship is a vital part of developing a repository's collections and preserving a community's identity.

---

## Accepting Donations

Step 1. In-House Paperwork and Collection Information

Gather basic information about a collection received from a donor to document authenticity and gain a better understanding of the materials' condition and scope. Complete an administrative form about the collection that includes: the name of the collection, a brief description of its contents, the name of the donor, the donor's relationship to the creator of the records, biographical information about the creator, disposition instructions (how the collection must be treated according to the donor's desires if the institution will seek to dispose of materials), provenance (history of who owned the collection and when), and the known holder of the collection's literary rights. It is useful to include a place on the form with the date the gift was acknowledged by a thank-you note.

Always remember to inquire of a donor about other records in his possession that might be of interest and may relate to what is being donated. Sometimes a valuable new collection is only one question away. Often donors do not realize the extent of materials they have that may be of interest to you: Sometimes even a casual conversation can lead to an additional donation.

In addition to seeking donations of archival material, do not be afraid to ask your donors for any additional necessary assistance. Provide information about the supplies needed to properly house their materials, and ask donors if they would be willing to provide a monetary contribution to help care for the donation.

Step 2. Formal Donor Agreement

In addition to the in-house paperwork to track the donation, have the donor sign a "donor agreement form" to make the transfer official. Include the donor's vital information, such as name and address. Most importantly, have the donor sign over intellectual and property rights. According to federal law, the intellectual ownership (known as the literary rights) of materials is transferred separately from the physical items. A donor agreement form must include a clause that transfers both physical and intellectual custody to an institution. Archives receiving donations of materials must have the copyright owner specifically sign over the intellectual property rights. Otherwise, anytime a researcher desires to publish from materials, they must seek permission from the donor or his surviving family and not from the housing institution itself. The ownership of copyright of archival materials resides with the creator of the materials or with the family if the creator is deceased. To have an owner sign over intellectual property rights, include a statement such as the following within a donor agreement form:

> *I assign and convey legal title and all literary property rights, which I may possess to the material described above to the Our Town Public Library. I agree that the Library may use the material as it seems most beneficial, with the exception of the restrictions or conditions stated above.*

Without this statement, for works created after January 1, 1978 (but before December 31, 2002), the copyright of materials remains with the family until 70 years after the author's death. If the work is published before December 31, 2002, its copyright is extended to 70 years after the author's death or to December 31, 2041 — whichever is greater. Works created between 1923 and 1977 have a copyright of up to 67 years. Materials created before 1923 are in the public domain.

There is currently a heavy debate and legal action over the future of copyright as we advance in the digital age. Copyright is subject to changes in legislation. All formal binding documents should be reviewed by a qualified attorney.

Step 3. Acknowledgment

Remember to acknowledge a donor's gift with a thank-you note. Include information on what is being done to handle the donation. If possible, tell donors when records will be processed, how they fit in with the rest of the collections, and how they are a valuable addition to the community. If appropriate, include information about how a separate monetary donation is being used to prolong the life of the materials.

---

## Model 5

### Collecting in a Rural Area:

### Churchill County Museum & Archives

The Churchill County Museum and Archives is the only repository in Fallon, Nevada (the only incorporated town in the county of Churchill). In 1986, *Life Magazine* coined the area's main thoroughfare, the Lincoln Highway (which predates Route 66 and served as the country's first transcontinental highway) "the loneliest road in America." The state seized this intended pejorative as a marketing slogan and the museum now calls itself "The Best Little Museum on Highway 50, the Loneliest Road in America." Established as a permanent repository in 1967 in an old Safeway building, the institution ties itself firmly to the culture of its region and makes itself a very visible presence in daily life.

Interest in establishing the museum grew in 1964 from the Nevada State centennial celebrations. Such celebrations are often an impetus for increased attention on historical records and artifacts around the world. Focused and successful follow-through on ideas deriving from festivities allowed Churchill County to create a cultural institution that sees itself as a multifaceted community resource: creating a comfortable environment for patrons, building collections that preserve local history, and developing programs and exhibits to boost education.

The museum was first run as a volunteer organization, but county officials recognized the institution's value and realized that such an operation needed full-time attention for success. They arranged for the collections to remain under private ownership in control of the museum's Friends group, which to date counts more than three hundred members. The county hired a full-time professional museum director and, later, nine part-time workers, while creating a budget for museum operations. With the guidance of a professional, the institution can balance the tasks of collecting, providing access, and education with continual outreach to ensure support.

With over two-thirds of its collections focusing on artifacts and with a staff trained in museum methods, the institution also collects archives as part of its mission. It serves as a repository for the oldest town and county records, offering a safe space for their storage, while simultaneously developing collections of personal papers such as diaries and correspondence. A grant program helped develop an oral history collection that highlights the stories of more than one hundred people and serves to fill gaps in the community record.

The Friends and museum staff work hard to raise outside money for support through other grants and fundraising efforts. This is appreciated by the government and boosts general goodwill. The institution promotes good community relations and "giving back" to its neighbors. It tries to make everyone feel welcome and stresses that it is the appropriate place to deposit items of local historical interest throughout the community. The museum director accomplishes this through face-to-face contact, as well as by being active on community committees, serving on state boards, working with the state's travel and tourism division, and creating written materials about collections and activities.

An accession committee meets once a month to review potential donations, allowing them to actively control items that are accessioned and ensuring that they conform to the museum's collections policy. Items that fall outside of their scope are turned away or referred to other appropriate repositories outside of town. While citizens are aware of the museum as the central place to bring historical items, the institution continually reaches out to its community to cultivate awareness of items and activities that relate to museum work. For example, recent construction on the local courthouse and a nearby road occurred near the location of a buried time capsule from the 1964 centennial celebration. Museum staff made sure to inform workmen about the time capsule and asked them to watch out for it. Indeed, the workmen struck the artifact while digging and brought it to the attention of the museum director immediately. In the past, it might have been discarded without a second thought.

Successfully documenting a community involves the cultural heritage professional seeking to persistently reach out to the populace to address potential donors and supporters. An institution with employees who make themselves visible, successfully explain the organization's purpose, and continually reemphasize their goals and value to the community can tie itself firmly to the locale's identity and help the institution become an entity that is well respected. Determined volunteers can work to raise awareness and help communities recognize that historical programs need to consider how to sustain themselves after they establish themselves. Employees need to keep these considerations continually perceptible.

## Outside Assistance

In cases where there is not a professional archivist on staff (and even when there is one), consultants or other outside help will be useful to jump-start a collaborative archives program. The consultant can make recommendations based on knowledge of other community archives and a learned understanding from assessing collections. Because of their objective viewpoints, consultants often have an advantage over insiders in recognizing problems related to the management of records and with an organization's collaborative partners. An outside advisor can help moderate the beginnings of collaborative work and can make suggestions for change more easily than one who may be extricated in the politics of a situation. The consultant with experience in running cooperative projects can help promote local records partnerships and can serve as a liaison, initiating proceedings between partnering colleagues. Consultants can help diverse organizations find neutral ground and can recommend approaches to archival projects that will benefit all parties involved.

An archives consultant may provide an assessment of an institution and its partner institutions. For such an assessment, a consultant will develop an overview that includes a general description of all partnering archival collections and discusses the role of each collection within its parent organization and community. This will help pave the way for the writing and rewriting of collection development policies and the creation of long-range plans. The consultant's assessment should provide a survey that identifies local record groups and series, while emphasizing strengths and weaknesses in documentation. The consultant will evaluate the current arrangement of collections with suggestions for alternate systems of organization through intellectual and physical control. She may evaluate current management tools and provide a description of other appropriate tools, including accession registers, policy and procedure manuals, finding aids, and automated databases. The information provided will allow the consultant or will help the institution to evaluate the organization's role in the archival community and prepare it for more effective collaboration. Finally, a consultant can provide training so that methods of archival management can be applied by staff when consulting services are no longer employed.

To perform an assessment, an institution should seek a consultant who has a broad-based background. You should employ an archivist with experience in different types of Archives. A consultant must be familiar with how to adapt to different situations. Such an archivist must understand how to adapt to differing institutional cultures and financial situations. The archivist must be flexible and see the reasonable prospects for an institution, no matter its circumstances. Consultants should ground theory and ideals with an ability to adjust to diverse situations. Often, institutions receive final consultant reports and instructions that seem far removed from what they are capable of accomplishing. Such written recommendations are often thrown in a drawer and never used as guides; consulting services were just a waste of both time and money. Make sure an archivist is able to tailor her approach to your needs.

Institutions wishing to employ a consultant should seek one with the appropriate education for archives management. This should be someone with a graduate degree in the field, which usually means an MS in library science or an MA in history. Either degree must be accompanied with a specialization in archiving. A consultant will charge by the hour, the day, or the project. Archival consultant fees range from $25 up to $100 or more per hour. This is dependent on what they can afford to charge, their skills, and their expertise. For example, if you want someone who specializes in automation, the cost may be higher than that of a generalist. To find an archivist, institutions generally put out a Request for Proposal (RFP) and ask professionals to bid on the project, seeking individuals with the most complete and least costly proposals. Many colleges and universities have specialized job listings online for people in this field where institutions can post RFPs. Or, you may advertise in local professional journals or obtain lists of archives consultants from historic records advisory boards or professional associations.

The contract you draw up with the consultant should include a summary of the project, the schedule for the work and its completion, what is expected of each party (the consultant and the client), and payment terms. The consultant may wish to retain title to the material she provides in the form of intellectual property rights so she can reuse the information and her wording of it in other reports that she provides to other clients, but organizations should be sure that the contract allows them to use the materials provided without any liens or encumbrances. Otherwise, they may be required to pay an additional fee to reproduce materials they wish to distribute in-house or for educational purposes. In the contract, institutions may also include an indemnity clause if the consultant is working with particularly valuable materials. The document should include signatures of the consultant and the executive on the client's end with the authority to make such contracts. It is worthwhile to have a lawyer look over the contract for the project, if one can be afforded.

A good consultant can train volunteers and nonprofessionals to implement basic archives processing. Many nonprofessionals also feel comfortable taking on more generalized management tasks and can learn to implement professional standards. Organizations that do not have professionals on staff or that do not have expertise in the area of archiving will require training to achieve any collecting goals that include management of records. Training offered specifically by a consultant is not necessary. Training can give an institution the focused attention it needs to swiftly move ahead with goals, but there are often other options available. Some professional institutions, such as boards of library commissioners, state Archives, and State Historical Records Advisory Boards (SHRABs), have experts available to visit repositories and provide some guidance. Volunteers and others can also get schooling by attending conferences and workshops hosted by professional associations.

A consultant with experience in archives and records management is beneficial for community projects, but this temporary consultant or another form of short-term assistance can only prod an archives management program along and cannot manage an extensive, long-range agenda. In the long term, every town should seek to hire a professional archivist to coordinate a full-blown, community-wide historic records plan. Most archives management programs that rely on temporary help to get a project started and do not plan to work toward hiring a permanent archivist will fail or fall short of far-reaching goals. Professionals in other fields (including librarians, who are more widely available than archivists in small towns) and volunteers can only give limited attention to sustaining an archival program. A consultant can help you better understand why you need an archivist and how archivists function. This will help the Archives make informed decisions about when it is appropriate to hire a permanent archivist and what to look for in a professional. A fully operational and successful archival program cannot be run on a shoestring and without someone at the helm who understands the field. For those who cannot afford a full-time archivist, consider hiring a permanent one on a part-time basis. Or, consider hiring a roving archivist for whom you can share the cost and who can work collaboratively to help other organizations in your town or area towns.[59]

## Funding for Archives Projects

Grant opportunities for hiring experts to visit and provide training is available and should be sought when additional funds are needed to bring in a professional. Repositories without a professional archivist on staff can use a consultant to quickly gain an understanding of a collection and prepare a plan for the repository to continue with inventories, arrangement, description, and preservation. Even when an institution is staffed by professionals, grants can be used for specialized projects that require unique knowledge or demand time that is just not available through an institution's normal channels. There are a number of federal organizations that provide funding for assistance. Grantors often encourage institutions to pursue collaborative projects, but always look for programs that they think will be successful. "The first step in developing a grants program is developing an organization and programs that will attract funding."[60]

One of the primary grantors for archives training, which often includes an element of surveying and processing, is the National Historical Publications and

---

59. See Model Six – "Traveling Archivist Program: Montana Historical Society" at the end of this section for more information.
60. Sarah Brophy, *Is Your Museum Grant-Ready: Assessing Your Organization's Potential for Funding* (Lanham, Maryland: AltaMira Press, 2005), 3. Brophy's book is an excellent resource for preparing your institution to seek funding.

Records Commission (NHPRC). This federal funding agency is affiliated with the National Archives and Records Administration (NARA). NHPRC assists archives through a network of state partners, working to preserve and make collections accessible and providing education to assist with the care of materials. They also provide funds for publishing historical records that are valuable in the understanding of American history.

NHPRC doles out a large portion of funds through State Historical Records Advisory Boards that evaluate local projects of various sizes and distribute money to successful grant applicants. By NHPRC regulation, SHRABs are run by State Historical Records Coordinators, who are members of the Council of State Archivists (CoSA). State archivists work collectively through CoSA to define and promote archival matters nationally, in addition to their local duties. Their work is intended "to ensure that the nation's documentary heritage is preserved and accessible."[61] Grant funding has been vital to their efforts, promoting both large- and small-scale projects that secure national historic treasures, as well as valued local archives that cement local culture and provide community value.

The Institute of Museum and Library Services (IMLS) is the nation's primary source of federal funds for museums and libraries. The Museum and Library Services Act of 1996 established IMLS within the National Endowment for the Humanities and mandated that the agency work to sustain cultural heritage and knowledge, enhance learning and innovation, support professional development, and enhance the public-service mission of libraries and museums. The agency provides a wide range of services, from supporting technical assistance for small institutions to supporting large-scale collaborative

---

61. From CoSA Web site (http://www.statearchivists.org).

partnerships. The agency was created in support of the idea that "libraries and museums help create vibrant, energized learning communities," which are necessary to propel a successful democracy. "Our role at the Institute is to provide leadership and funding for the nation's museums and libraries, resources these institutions need to fulfill their mission of becoming centers of learning for life crucial to achieving personal fulfillment, a productive workforce, and an engaged citizenry."[62]

The National Endowment for the Humanities also offers funding for archival repositories through its Preservation Assistance Grants for Smaller Institutions. It provides monetary support so institutions may hire consultants to assist with professional needs, including, but not limited to, archival surveys, building assessments, training, and equipment. The endowment helps primarily small and mid-size institutions by providing grants to assist with the preservation and care of diverse documentary materials related to the humanities.[63]

The Save America's Treasures Grant Program is a public/private partnership through the National Park Service and the National Trust for Historic Preservation. It supports the preservation or conservation of nationally significant documents, artifacts, works of art, historic structures, and sites. The Save America's Treasures program was established by executive order in 1998 in anticipation and commemoration of the new millennium. The program aims to save cultural artifacts, educate Americans about issues related to the preservation of cultural resources, develop pride in our heritage and

---

62. From the IMLS Web site (http://www.imls.gov/about/about.shtm).
63. Information about Preservation Assistance Grants for Smaller Institutions from NEH on its Web site (http://www.neh.gov/grants/guidelines/pag.html).

concern for its safekeeping, and encourage involvement in preservation efforts.[64]

The Conservation Assessment Program (CAP) is another fund that offers assistance for the management of collections. It supports general museum evaluations that consider environmental conditions, staffing and training, building construction, and museum policies and procedures. Professionals perform a two- to three-day assessment that aims to help museums develop better strategies for collections care. The short assessment serves as a tool for long-range planning and fundraising. CAP is supported through a cooperative agreement with Heritage Preservation, and the Institute of Museum and Library Services.[65]

The Council on Library and Information Resources developed "Cataloging Hidden Special Collections and Archives" in 2008. Supported by the Andrew W. Mellon Foundation, the program seeks to support collections with national significance that possess value for scholarship and teaching. It involves adopting standard technologies that will make valuable collections more accessible.[66]

Nonprofit institutions may also find financial support for collections through philanthropic foundations that support the preservation of cultural heritage. There are large foundations supporting a wide range of projects, as well as small and medium-sized organizations that may

---

64. Information from the Save America's Treasures Web site (http://www.preservationnation.org/travel-and-sites/save-americas-treasures/). At the time of this writing, the federal government has threatened to eliminate funding for this program. Grant money is often vital to the protection of our archives, but its availability is tenuous.
65. Information about the CAP program from its Web site (http://www.heritagepreservation.org/cap/index.html). For more about Heritage Preservation, see its Web site (http://www.heritagepreservation.org/ABOUTHP/INFO.HTM).
66. Information from "Cataloging Hidden Special Collections and Archives" proposal to Andrew W. Mellon Foundation (http://www.clir.org/hiddencollections/HiddenCatFinal.pdf).

focus their grant efforts on a particular subject or geographic area. Information about foundations is gathered by a nonprofit agency called the Foundation Center. This agency believes that philanthropy is the key to a democratic society and aims to connect nonprofits with potential supporters. "Established in 1956 and today supported by close to 550 foundations, the Foundation Center is a national nonprofit service organization recognized as the nation's leading authority on organized philanthropy, connecting nonprofits and the grant makers supporting them to tools they can use and information they can trust."[67]

The Foundation Center has teamed with the Library of Congress to cull 2,270 grants specifically aimed at cultural heritage institutions from a general grants database of more than 22,000 grants. The partnership's *Foundation Grants for Preservation in Libraries, Archives and Museums* is available online and can be easily searched for funding opportunities to assist your archives management goals.[68]

Institutions considering applying for grants must be organized and prepared to demonstrate their efficiency and potential for follow-through on what they propose in their grant applications. They must also have a plan for sustaining programs once grants are completed. Having proper administrative documents in place, including such materials as a mission statement and collection development policy, are basic elements required by most funders as an initial step. The success of the grant is highly dependent on administrative support for the archives

---

67. About the Foundation Center (http://foundationcenter.org/about).
68. *Foundation Grants for Preservation in Libraries, Archives and Museums* (http://www.loc.gov/preserv/foundtn-grants.pdf).

program.[69] Local authorities responsible for funding include nonprofit boards, local governments, and private administrators that must support and understand the value of archives. Before the grant process and as part of it, repositories must make clear internally how well-managed archives benefit the community, patrons, and the institutions of which they are a part. The funder wants to see that an organization is not dependent on it for support but has ongoing support of its own that will ensure the funder's supplemental money is put to good use.

---

69. A study assessing why some NHPRC grant programs thrive while others whither was discussed by David M. Wienberg in "The Impact of Grantsmaking: An Evaluation of Archival and Records Management Programs at the Local Level," *The American Archivist* 62 (Fall 1999): 247–270.

**Web Sites for Funding Agencies**

Council of State Archivists (CoSA)
http://www.statearchivists.org/

Council on Library and Information Resources (CLIR) – "Cataloging Hidden Special Collections and Archives"
http://www.clir.org/hiddencollections/index.html

Heritage Preservation – Conservation Assessment Program (CAP)
http://www.heritagepreservation.org/CAP/application.html

Institute of Museum and Library Services (IMLS)
http://www.imls.gov/about/about.shtm

National Endowment for the Humanities (NEH) – Preservation Assistance Grants
http://www.neh.gov/grants/guidelines/pag.html

National Historical Publications and Records Commission (NHPRC) http://www.archives.gov/nhprc/about

National Park Services – Save America's Treasures Grant Program
http://www.nps.gov/history/hps/treasures/

Foundation Grants for Preservation in Libraries, Archives and Museums
http://www.loc.gov/preserv/foundtn-grants.pdf

## Model 6

## Traveling Archivist Program:

## Montana Historical Society

Montana's culture and geography encourage collaboration. According to state archivists, no one has enough money to do everything they want to do, so Montanans understand that working together benefits everyone, with larger organizations helping smaller ones. An IMLS census project recently located only twenty-two self-identified archivists in the state of Montana.[70] For an area that's more than 700 miles wide, where towns can easily be an hour or more from the next nearest settlement, the difficulty for cooperative archives projects lies in how to get professional help from more populous regions into remote areas.

The Montana State Historical Records Advisory Board embarked on a "traveling archivist" program in 2000 through an NHPRC grant that it hoped to parlay into an ongoing project. Using contact information gathered through a cooperative project with the Museums Association of Montana to create a directory of cultural heritage repositories in the state, the SHRAB notified these organizations that, through its grant, it was available to those in need of archival assistance. The traveling archivist program required interested institutions to first perform self-assessments. They were asked to evaluate collecting policies, forcing repositories to think about how they were

---

70. See A*Census online (http://www.archivists.org/a-census).

going to build collections even before professional help arrived on-site.

A full-time archivist was hired to tour the state, spending up to one month at an institution to provide assistance and then moving on to another repository. Repositories provided in-kind support in the form of housing for the traveling archivist, who could not reasonably help more than one town at a time due to geography. This turned out to be one of the biggest drawbacks to the program. It was difficult to keep a full-time archivist busy. Most of the repositories the traveling archivist visited were run by volunteers who were not available during all the hours professional assistance was on hand. The archivist, therefore, had idle time.

The program did not turn out exactly the way it was planned, but it was considered a great learning experience and helped build relationships between cultural heritage repositories. The impracticality of employing a full-time person to travel caused state archivists to reevaluate goals. Looking back, the archivists see the project as the foundation of a continual outreach effort that draws together repositories, provides opportunities for building strong collections, encourages professionalism, and persistently looks for collaborative opportunities to strengthen efforts.

Annual NHPRC grants support workshops and conferences that allow archivists to collaborate with professional librarians and museum personnel. This funding has also been put toward producing a semiannual newsletter that helps maintain contact with repositories across the state. Since the original grant, cross-professional colleagues have developed listservs to maintain contact. Collaborative cataloging projects have also grown through networking efforts. The Northwest Digital Archives and the Montana Memory Project are programs that have provided archivists with an opportunity to be more visible in the

Montana community. These programs help provide access to information about materials, but they also give the archivists an outlet to stress the importance of properly maintaining collections. They aim to stress that preservation is primary and digitization is secondary. The Montana County History Initiative is a recent project that has focused on communities celebrating centennials, aiming to raise awareness of cultural heritage and pride in community, with an ulterior motive to preserve materials.

A current NHPRC grant is allowing the idea of the "traveling archivist" to continue through a student archivist program. During the summer, a student from the Western Washington University Archives and Records Management program trains at the Montana Historical Society Research Center for a week, then spends the next seven weeks in a repository, assisting with archives. This year the project will be expanded to include students from the University of Wisconsin—Milwaukee. The program is an opportunity for students to perform hands-on archives work, helps repositories, and serves as an outreach initiative for Montana. This outreach effort aims to encourage students to settle and work in the state, bringing their archival expertise with them.

In Montana, word of mouth is vital. Archivists work to build trust through collaborative efforts and by continually trying new things to help communities. All their successes have built upon each other. They have sometimes had to scale back goals, but they do what they can with what they have, and they accomplish a lot. The key, they say, is to get yourself out there. Let people know what you are doing and why to build the support that leads to success.

## Community Documentation Strategy Adapted for LAM

Archivists developed the "community documentation strategy" to address the issue of how institutions could best work toward the construction of a thorough documentary record about a given subject. It focuses on institutions that create records and aims to have them work collaboratively with other related organizations to preserve collections with interconnected themes. The principles of the strategy can be valuable to multifaceted cultural heritage institutions interested in preserving and promoting local history. Applying some basic principles of the community documentation strategy requires those collecting historical resources to collaborate with each other and with those who create and use their collections to determine the full scope of a community's history.

Though originally focused on archives in particular, the basics of a comprehensive documentation approach can be expanded to include all elements of material culture. Using these methods, repositories work together to define a collecting scope by evaluating their community and its components. They then seek historical materials in all formats related to the aspects of their community that they determine should be documented and preserved. This strategy can be an overarching framework for collecting programs and can be a launching point for each repository to create a collection development policy. It serves as a bond to promote community identity and interests. It is a very active way of ensuring that bits of history are not lost to time. Archivist Larry Hackman explains:

> *A documentation strategy is a plan to assure the adequate documentation of an ongoing issue, activity, function, or subject. The strategy is*

> *ordinarily designed, promoted, and in part implemented by an ongoing mechanism involving archival documentation creators, record administrators, archivists, users, other experts, and beneficiaries and other interested parties. The documentation strategy is carried out through the mutual efforts of many institutions and individuals influencing the creation and management of records and the retention and archival accessioning of some of them. The strategy is regularly refined in response to changing conditions as reflected in available information expertise and opinions. Strategies may be developed at levels ranging from worldwide and nationwide to statewide and communitywide.* [71]

A comprehensive documentation strategy encourages participants to identify the events, people, and places that made up the history of a given topic.[72] This strategy is extremely thorough and provides us with a useful way to think about what we are doing, even if the strategy is not implemented in full and only pieces are used to help develop inclusive collections. Few communities have attempted to use such a comprehensive tool for reviewing their collections. If a community does not want to implement the full program outlined here, it will find

---

71. Larry J. Hackman provides the most succinct definition of the documentation strategy I have read in "The Documentation Strategy Process: A Model and a Case Study," *The American Archivist* 50 (Winter 1987): 14. Hackman's collaborative article with Joan Warnow-Blewett thoroughly explains the strategy and offers the documentation project of the American Institute of Physics as a shining example of the strategy put to use. See the Center for the History of Physics' Web site (http://www.aip.org/history).
72. Hans Booms talks about the nature of and purpose of understanding these societal relationships in "Society and the Formation of a Documentary Heritage: Issues in the Appraisal of Archival Sources," *Archivaria* 24 (Summer 1987): 103. Schellenberg also discusses this in his "Appraisal of Modern Public Records."

components that will assist with collecting goals and collaboration.

Community documentation principles may encourage some repositories to reevaluate their missions, viewing themselves as organizations that document history rather than solely as collectors of records or other material resources. Appreciating the wide range of cultural heritage resources we discussed earlier and understanding the many people who manage historical records allows us to think of our own collections in a broader context. Repositories should focus on an understanding of the context in which materials are collected, created, and administered, and the many ways they benefit society. Community documentation partners must define the topic they wish to document, and then evaluate the makeup of the materials related to the topic. Collections of all sorts can be reevaluated with this principle in mind.

Significantly, like archivists, museum professionals are looking beyond "conventional museum functions [in order] to encompass overall community development." The museum has a role to play in reflecting a locale's sense of self, boosting pride and reinforcing community "solidarity."[73] By focusing a collection on the artifacts created by a particular society, the museum enmeshes itself into that culture and becomes a prime force in communicating the ideals of its people. "As museums are becoming more people- and community-centered (rather than object-centered), and concerned with people's living culture and not just their past, they are being liberated from 'the romanticism…of the decontextualized object.'"[74] A

---

73. Christina F. Kreps, *Liberating Culture Cross-Cultural Perspectives on Museums, Curation and Heritage Preservation.* (London: Routledge, 2003): 114. Kreps discusses non-Western museums reflecting a sense of local culture through collections. Her observations about museums' abilities to build community are particularly well-suited to the community documentation strategy.

74. Kreps, 148.

community documentation project within the museum environment ties itself directly to a goal of community reflection. Museums have developed their own participatory approaches to encourage their institution's community involvement. These methods of developing collections and boosting the institution's cultural role complement the community documentation strategy developed by archivists.

Libraries have always regarded themselves as community centers to one degree or another. Citizens see their libraries as hubs of information and, as such, libraries have been given great community standing and have received donations of great historical import. Ensconced in local culture, libraries are able to play a mediator role in a community documentation project, bringing their own collections to the table and encouraging a strong patron base to join efforts. Generally possessing valued public buildings, libraries can also contribute this space as neutral ground for collaborative meetings.

To begin a community documentation project, collaborators must establish a committee consisting of professionals and individuals with diverse expertise related to the collecting of cultural heritage resources. This group will be made up of the collaborating partners identified earlier in this book. The collaborative should first aim to enlist representatives from major historical repositories collecting in their chosen focus area. These institutions will likely include libraries, historical societies, museums, and university archives. Town clerks, records managers, and other quasi-cultural heritage professionals may also participate at this point if they have a desire and understanding of documentation work. Otherwise, they may be brought in a bit later as the project proceeds.

Representatives must work together to consider what defining aspects and specific elements of their topic should be documented. They should approach specialists in a variety of areas to join the group and provide insight about their respective fields to ensure that all appropriate details are documented. The creation of a community documentation plan impels us to call on people outside of the cultural heritage fields who have various expertise within society to develop collections that adequately reflect society's makeup. The famous German archivist Hans Booms, renowned for his archival work and consideration of techniques and theories for archives management, stated that:

> *The documentation plan…should not remain the responsibility of a single or even several archivists. The plan should be the product of a procedure characterized by both a division of labour* [sic] *and cooperation among workers. Wherever possible, it should be subject to the criticism of a team. If at all possible, it should be discussed in an advisory council composed of individuals from different areas of life such as administration, science, the media or economics. It should be written down, if possible published, but in any case it should be included as part of the documentary heritage itself.*[75]

The plan itself will discuss the complete range of documentation necessary to describe and provide a full representation of a given topic. "One must understand the political, economic, social and cultural milieu of any given society to understand its archives."[76] Group members should devise a timeline listing important events. It should discuss the people, organizations, and places that define a

---

75. Booms, 106.
76. Terry Cook, "Archival Science and Postmodernism: New Formulations for Old Concepts," *Archival Science* 1.1 (2000): 3–24.

community. Once the groundwork is established by considering the community and aspects of it that should be documented, a collaborative group should evaluate available existing documentation by reviewing (or conducting) record surveys, inventories, and an individual institution's collection development policies. This knowledge can be used to actively shape collections, define an individual organization's niches, and target records to be collected.[77]

When embarking on a local community documentation project, an informational session should be held for the public to include them in the process and encourage identification of significant materials that are held outside of major repositories. One way to spread the word about a community documentation project is to hold a public informational session that invites citizens to learn about the local documentation work that cultural heritage institutions are undertaking and how to care for archives. You can send out invitations to the event to select people, as well as advertise through posters, brochures, and articles in the local newspaper. It is a good idea to encourage residents to bring some of their valued treasures to an informational session. People are often excited to talk about their family memorabilia and provide information about their documentation in a spirit of cooperation or to elicit preservation information to care for the items they hold dear. An introductory session can help a documentation committee better comprehend the extent of existing materials outside of repositories. It is important to focus first on gathering information about records available without aiming to acquire donations. People who are approached to donate records without a full understanding

---

77. A guide listing elements of comprehensive community documentation plans and sample questions for evaluating community documentation are provided at the end of this section.

of collection development, cultural heritage, and a community documentation project often feel cornered and back away.

Many individuals who move out of a town may take noteworthy collections with them. It is important to try to contact these people, too. They are best identified and located by townspeople who were friendly with them and know where they relocated. Ask those who attend an introductory meeting to identify such people. Determine what documentation related to the community has been removed from it.

Those without "expertise" in a particular field can also provide valuable insight for a documentation strategy. Community members invited to an informational session can be asked for their insight regarding what makes their community important to them. People may then see their personal experiences in a larger context — as part of local culture and a larger regional and national psyche. The fabric of history is made up of personal stories, and getting the input of those whose stories should be reflected in our archives is important to ensure that all of society is well documented.

Because it involves people from many backgrounds, a community documentation strategy requires a stronger collaborative effort than "traditional" collection development. "Each documentation strategy molds its program to meet the particular problems posed by the environment being documented."[78] While the elements of each documentation plan may be similar, and the original questions that one asks to evaluate the documentation itself may be used across communities, you must recognize that every community is different and, therefore, every strategy must be specially designed for its particular collaborative.

---

[78] Phillip N. Alexander and Helen Samuels. "The Roots of 128: A Hypothetical Documentation Strategy," *The American Archivist* 59 (Fall 1987): 530.

A predetermined model cannot be used to help document community. Every documentation group must ensure that its vision melds with that of its citizens and adequately reflects the ideals of the culture with which it is involved. Working collaboratively, individuals with broad perspectives will ensure that appropriate aspects of their society are considered, and then properly recorded and preserved.

Though a large documentation committee can do the work of brainstorming what to include in the documentation plan, the plan itself should be written by fewer people. A small group or an individual from the committee can elicit ideas from the general members and then formalize them in a written document. Using methodical steps for documenting a community will greatly assist with its goals and their achievement. Partners must ensure that ideas are written and sorted, providing a clear path for documentation work.

Documentation is a continual process, but the time taken for listing appropriate areas for initial exploration should not be indefinite. The group must determine how it will know when it has defined all of the areas needing representation in the collections. Lists may be refined in the future, but the process of preliminary listing, brainstorming, and evaluating missing resources based on surveys must have a stopping point. The collaborative may set a deadline for this preliminary work to end. Before the plan is written, the core group should establish time limits for the completion of general research, planning, and writing of necessary collection development policies. They should help define documentation milestones that can be written into the strategy and make plans for actively reviewing strides toward effective documentation.[79] Timelines

---

79. One of the most effective uses of the documentation strategy to date is the program instituted by the American Institute of Physics as summarized in Larry Hackman and

providing organizations with realistic periods in which to finish necessary work should be incorporated.

It is unrealistic to expect repositories that are busy with such tasks as processing existing collections, creating exhibits, and serving researchers to focus fully on documentation work in a short period. Yet the basic deadlines should also not be too far into the future, pushing the project off longer than necessary. After initial work, organizations may then go on to spend most of their time actively seeking records and personal papers related to their identified gaps. Collaboration must become a core function of each institution's goals for it to be successful, and, therefore, it must be juggled with other core functions.

As a project progresses, it should be continually evaluated and revised. Many collaborative projects have a strong start and then are abandoned or slowly lose attention when the initial work is completed. "All too often documentation efforts are treated only as projects, by definition not ongoing. Preservation work and other activities that may need to extend over decades are not carried out, and the experience of the project is not built into ongoing efforts."[80] Collaboration must be continuing. It should carry on even in the face of adversity. Collaborative members should be encouraged to report on activities. They should communicate accordingly to keep

---

Joan Warnow-Blewett's article "The Documentation Strategy Process: A Model and a Case Study," *The American Archivist* 50 (Winter 1987): 12–47. A complete report of the project was written by Joan Warnow-Blewett, Joel Genuth, and Spencer R. Weart as *Documenting Multi-Institutional Collaborations* (American Institute of Physics, 2001), and is available at http://www.aip.org/history/pubs/collabs/mainreport.pdf. AIP has built case studies, fieldwork, and evaluation into its documentation planning. The institute has made it a part of its standard approach to study how records are created and how well plans are implemented. Its objectives are six-fold: 1. To locate documents; 2. To preserve them; 3. To create oral histories and conduct interviews; 4. To organize information and create indices; 5. To conduct outreach and educate interested parties about records; 6. To promote records for research. Those interested in pursuing a full-blown documentation strategy should read the summary article.

80. Hackman and Warnow-Blewett, 36.

progressing and to avoid misunderstandings. The group should continually inform the public about its progress, regularly reaching out to inform record creators about the importance of the materials they create. This will ensure persistent care for records and the never-ending development of the documentary record.

Furthermore, continuing collaborative work will ensure that as the community changes and evolves, the documentation that is preserved to represent it will also advance appropriately. A documentation strategy is not a static plan: It should be continually reexamined to assess how appropriately it reflects society, its citizens, and the ideals of its cultural heritage partners. The strategy opens the door for institutions wishing to undertake supplemental large-scale ventures (such as oral history projects) by identifying which areas are most in need of documentation and encouraging diverse systems of recording information as society changes.

Proponents of documentation strategies have described varying methods for evaluating culture and determining what resources to keep that reflect society. There are opponents of documentation strategies who say that most people handling archival collections do not have the time or resources to enact such a strategy and that it is more realistic to come up with processes to evaluate offered collections. However, without understanding what others are collecting, evaluating what resources are available, and determining your niche for collecting in the archival community, collection development is ineffectual, and the value of a particular collection is obscure.

It is important for a repository to continually collaborate with outside organizations to build collections and create a strong documentary record. We need to identify the groups with which we share commonalities, a sense of purpose, and a collecting focus. This allows us to develop methodical ways of gathering information resources and primary-source material that take into account those with whom we can build collecting strategies. There is a mistaken belief among many researchers that repositories automatically create comprehensive collections that thoroughly provide evidence of society's activities and that it is just up to the researcher to locate where records are conscientiously stored. Unfortunately, this is not usually the case, unless institutions work diligently on collaborative collection development.

The techniques of the community documentation strategy offer us valuable tools for examining our communities, ensuring a broad perspective on our histories that is inclusive of all members of our society. The strategy also propels institutions to work together, which is a vital element to help ensure the longevity of cultural heritage institutions. A cultural heritage professional's work is never done. We are forever striving to reach an ideal, whether it is in collection management, description, or preservation. The community documentation strategy gives us a framework for examining our collecting scope and allows us to imagine our ideal collection. The next section discusses the theories that assist us with collection development decision-making and help us determine which specific records should be included in our planning.[81]

---

81. For a detailed analysis of the archive profession's use and views about the documentation strategy, see Doris J. Malkmus, "Documentation Strategy: Mastodon or Retro-Success," *The American Archivist* 71 (Fall/Winter 2008): 384–409.

## Elements of a Community Documentation Plan

1. Date of Project

2. Scope of the Project — Discuss the geographical area or topic upon which collaborative collection development is based.

3. Documentation Group — List collaborative participants in the project. Include individuals and their titles or roles in the community. List names of institutions involved in their current collecting focuses, and the formats of materials that they collect (e.g., archives, artifacts, publications).

4. What the Documentation for the Community Ideally Should Include — Create a timeline and a list of questions that relate to the project scope. Working as a group, consider important local historical events, people, organizations, and places. Representative "experts" from the various fields must take part. The goal is to list all of the different aspects that define what the community is and how it became that way.

5. Existing Documentation Quality — An extensive archives survey (which is described in detail later in this book) allows institutions to evaluate existing documentation quality and to better understand the records in their possession and those of their collaborative partners. Additionally, project members should review their own finding aids (if they have them) and other sources that describe what is currently

housed in their collections to help identify available resources. Identify subject areas for which there is strong documentation. Determine if the types of materials representing topics are in formats that best reflect their subjects. Determine if artifacts, records, and publications are available for various subjects.

6. Topical Areas That Are Under-documented — Work to ensure that topics that define the character of the community are represented. Review documentation about the most visible aspects of the community, as well as the more commonplace aspects that shape society but may not gain the same notoriety as others. List specific topics that are not represented in the documentation.

7. Actions Including Priorities for Collecting — Every aspect of society that is defined within the timeline will require documentation. Based on the identification of areas already documented, areas under-documented, and the discussion of what the documentation should ideally include, set priorities for collecting. Identify important topics. Identify appropriate formats for retaining information about subjects. Identify organizations currently collecting in given areas and those willing to develop collections in other areas if necessary.

8. Possible Information Sources — The group may need to consult additional individuals with subject knowledge. Also, particular record-holders may not have been identified at the outset and should now be included. Determine if any records have left the

community. Search for missing materials in online databases and on online auction sites such as eBay. Identify people who may have moved or otherwise left the community with important records. Identify ways to reach out to records creators and collectors. Define outreach opportunities.

9. Target Date for Review of Work and Project Revisions — During review, participants should determine collecting progress that has been made and cite any challenges (e.g., records related to a particular organization that have been discovered or destroyed). Participants will also want to note new areas for documentation that were not previously defined.

10. Collection Development Policies — Project participants should revise collection development policies within their own institutions based on group work. The policies may then be added to the group's community documentation plan so that group members can easily refer to them when necessary.

---

---

**Sample Questions for Evaluating Community Documentation**

Focus on one topic at a time from your timeline and compare existing documentation to an ideal that fully reflects the topic. This will help determine collecting priorities and plans.

- What is the topic?
- Why is this topic important?
- What does the existing historical documentation about this subject tell us about our community?
- What are the important people, places, institutions, and events associated with this topic?
- Does this topic relate to any other topics included in the documentation strategy?
- Who has created historical resources related to this topic?
- What historical resources for this topic are held in participating repositories?
- What historical resources for this topic are held outside of our community?

- What materials related to this topic are missing from the historical record? Can we locate them? Have they been destroyed?
- What individuals within our community might have information about this topic?
- What individuals outside of the community might have information about this topic?
- Do the resources related to this topic that we have identified offer multiple points of view? How can we ensure that all points of view are represented?
- Who are the experts on this topic? What do they think of the available documentation in this area?
- What are the possible audiences for this material?
- Can we create additional documentation related to this topic to make the historical record more complete (e.g, oral histories, photo-documentation projects)?

---

## Model 7

## Focused Documentation within a Locale:

## Marist College, New York

The Marist College Archives and Special Collections was started in 2000 and has become one of the premier repositories of environmental history in the country. When the head of Archives and Special Collections was hired to care for the school's archives and personal papers, he quickly realized the value of a group of documents that was gathered and donated to the college by an interested citizen. In the 1960s, the resident began collecting materials related to what is now called the "Scenic Hudson Decision," involving a proposed hydroelectric plant in the area where the individual's family and ancestors had lived for three hundred years. These materials would become the core of Marist's most unique and outstanding collection.

> *The Scenic Hudson Decision was a seventeen-year legal dispute which defeated Consolidated Edison's plan to embed the world's largest pumped storage hydroelectric plant into the face of Storm King Mountain, near Cornwall, New York. The lengthy and controversial case had an immense impact on environmental and legal issues affecting the Hudson River Valley as well as the nation. The landmark case set important precedents in environmental law including: the right of citizens to participate in environmental disputes, the emergence of environmental law as a legal specialty, ideas Congress incorporated in the country's first National Environment Policy Act (NEPA), federal*

> *and state regulation of the environment, and it is credited with launching the modern environmental movement.* [82]

When the archivist began work in the school, based in an upstate New York municipality of more than 600,000 people and located in the Hudson River Valley, he realized that no repository was thoroughly exploring the environmental history of the area and was concerned that existing documentation would be lost. Many cultural heritage caretakers tend to discount records being created today when developing collections and seek older materials to describe their chosen subject. The volume of materials produced in our society also makes it difficult to keep track of contemporary events and to ensure that the most vital records of activities are retained. The Marist Archives and Special Collections made a conscious decision to try to collect documentation related to a significant modern-day issue so it would not be lost or forgotten.

The repository started by contacting area libraries and institutions to inquire if anyone possessed materials relating to Hudson environmental history. The institution then applied for and received grant funding to perform a survey that allowed it to more systematically collect information about available documentation. To date, Marist has acquired twelve or more grants to develop and preserve their collection, while also recording information about similar collections so that it can keep track of the Hudson River Valley's full range of environmental documentation and can refer researchers interested in the topic. This work has allowed Marist to network with diverse people involved with conservation in the area; it has developed good cooperative relationships with various organizations.

---

82. Marist Environmental History Project, "The Scenic Hudson Decision" (http://library.marist.edu/archives/mehp/scenicedecision.html).

Early on, the Archives created a timeline of events using secondary sources about the Storm King case. It helped them learn about potential holders of additional environmental records. They persistently reached out to the community to see who had records related to the area's environmental movement, using the timeline as a guide for collecting, and approaching both organizations and individuals with ties to the environmental movement.

Many contacted libraries were preliminarily surprised at the things that interested Marist, but seeing the archivists' initial enthusiasm made them more aware and respectful of Hudson-related items in their holdings. Sometimes people offered to donate things to Marist's collection; at other times, Marist's Archives provided tips on how to keep materials safe where they were. They always emphasized the importance of what they were surveying and told people that the Archives was always available to give advice if needed. They provided the collection caretakers they addressed with information about available grant funding for the preservation of materials and sometimes even provided preservation supplies to help those who would have difficulty affording or acquiring them.

The project has been very successful providing a strong view of the Hudson River Valley's environmental history, and the program has reached the point where people come to Marist knowing they have papers and sometimes offering them additional materials. When collections are offered outside of their scope, they have helped place items at more appropriate repositories. The Marist Archives and Special Collections continues to actively seek materials about the Hudson River and supplements existing documentation with an oral history project. They also maintain a small collection of artifacts related to their topic.

The Archives tries to document the environmental story from all angles, but it has been difficult to get information from those who were against environmental protections in the Hudson River Valley. Therefore, the collection's strength lies in the telling of the environmentalist side. To try to round out perspectives, the Archives relies on secondary sources — writings about events and contemporary scientific reports. In one case, the Archives even found a report shelved in a library in a neighboring county through an online catalog and asked if they could add it to the Marist collection. The library gladly deaccessioned it because it was of little value to them as a single item; they recognized the greater value it held for the Hudson collection.

The Marist example demonstrates that with resources unavailable to some, a college archives can serve as a documentation hub, developing strong collections and assisting others with the preservation of vital community resources. The Marist College Archives and Special Collections is a model for such collaboration and a premier example of putting the community documentation strategy to work to ensure that the documentation related to a particular subject is surveyed, examined, and protected for future generations.

# 3. The Practice of Collection Development

Societies have developed collections as by-products of their communities' ideals. Western societies have until recently gathered books, artifacts, and archives subjectively — to reflect current tastes, to promote contemporary morals, and to engage the public in prearranged conversations begun by those with authority. In the last century and a half, ideas about the significance of the freethinking individual in a democratic society, the increased desire to understand varied cultures, and an emphasis on education of "the masses" has encouraged the development of professional and objective methods for the care and growth of collections. Today, we value diversity in the materials we retain. Rather than collecting in areas that promote elite ideals alone, we work to establish a well-rounded historical record represented by such things as book collections that cater to the reader of the novel as well as the scholar, and museums with artifacts created by fine artists sitting alongside more common objects reflecting an individual's life. All of these collections preserve ideas from all facets of society and form a documentary record that considers multiple strata of people and activities. However, because it is impossible to collect everything, we must use our own best judgment when making decisions about what to keep. Our conclusions can be informed by the past experiences of our colleagues. With a little knowledge of theory, you can more easily develop a strategy for collecting that is straightforward and sound, allowing the developer of collections to remain as objective as possible.

The foundation of archives collection development is theory that has been developed for more than a century. This theory makes us reflect on the nature of our materials, judging what documents are important for us to collect and what can be discarded. This chapter begins with a brief discussion of the evolution of theories in archives management so that institutions can better understand and thus more easily care for the records in their repositories. The description of the progression leads the reader to the development of the community documentation strategy so that he can better understand how to implement it. Following the discussion of theory, the chapter offers steps for creating a collection development plan, information about how to write a mission statement, guidelines for appraisal, guidelines for deaccessioning to support collection development, and steps for conducting an archival survey to support collection development.

You can justify keeping just about anything: It is much more difficult to come up with a reason to not keep something. This can only properly be done through the use of planning documents already in place to assist with new, incoming collections. Collection development and appraisal cannot be done without forethought about the purpose of the collecting body. The archivist must always keep that purpose in mind, taking into account the overall scope of the collection and the future direction of the Archives' activities to help it remain accountable to the organization's mission. We can rely only on the materials that survive to form our interpretations of the past. It is up to the cultural heritage professional to ensure that materials that best shed light on society are those that last. "All we can know about the past is what has survived, and what has survived is just an infinitesimally small portion of the evidence."[83] Our decisions about what to keep and the thoroughness of our actions irrevocably shape the documentary record.

As noted in the last chapter, all collecting organizations should work to develop the concept of a networked repository whose collecting goals are wound up with other collectors and the community's best interests. Consider an institution as part of a larger network within town. Consider what the institution has and what it would like to have. Consider how an organization fits within a larger group of cultural heritage institutions. Review your collections to determine what materials are missing from the piece of the story that the repository wants to tell about its community. Identify what materials would enhance your collections and be prepared to determine if such records exist. When we understand what aspects of history our collections do not reflect, we can better target and seek assistance from individuals who can help us locate missing information. We may also develop projects to create documentary heritage materials, such as oral histories, to fill gaps.

The current basis of care for our historical resources has been to try to provide separate homes for materials of diverse media, to develop separate professional techniques and standards to ensure their preservation, and to aid the accessibility of the information such resources contain about our cultural heritage. Because of the disparate nature of cultural heritage materials, it often makes sense to harbor items separately, yet it is time to break down some of our philosophical borders and see all culturally based collections as products of a civilized society that could be promoted together to benefit mankind — whether artifact, publication, or archival material.

---

83. Archibald, 53.

Over the past couple of decades, organizations have been moving toward melding collections "intellectually." Recently, much effort has been expended toward establishing intellectual control of related items, which involves developing digitized catalogues or finding aids that allow us to consider all materials related to a particular subject — whether artifact, publication, or archive. Less has been done to meld the collection development practices of the cultural heritage professions. We show in our databases all resources we possess related to a subject, but many do not work to make sure all aspects of that subject are being addressed or collected in the first place. By focusing on the practice of collection development, this chapter aims to assist the collection caretaker to first consider the whole collection itself before describing its individual parts.

## Collection Development and Appraisal Theory

Appraisal is the most complicated aspect of archival work and is tied most closely to collection development. It is the process of determining specifically which records should be kept for posterity to enhance the documentary record. Appraisal work should be directly based on an institution's collection development policy. However, the decision about which actual records should be chosen (the appraisal process) is controversial in that it is a subjective task based on various theories created by archivists. Some of the theories have grown from others, and some stand in direct contradiction to one another. The field of appraisal continues to evolve. Archivists try to base their appraisal decisions on theory and on common sense about what works for their particular collections. The following section discusses how and why appraisal theory has changed over the past century to make methods understandable so that nonprofessionals may more confidently apply them to collection decisions. "The selection of records of enduring value is the archivist's first responsibility. All other archival activities hinge on the ability to select wisely..."[84]

Archives professionals have progressed from passive caretakers of materials to active developers of collections that aim to document a wide range of human experiences, which can be supported by the highly hands-on community documentation strategy. Early on, archivists cared for records, but their role did not include gathering collections that reflected society. The historians were regarded as the true professionals and the archivists as supporting staff. The view of the profession has changed in accordance with the way modern society values information. With the proliferation of materials and an abundance of recorded documentation, the archivist is needed to provide organized access to records documenting a broader interpretation of human experience than previously thought important. Based on familiarity with theories of archival management and experience with collection development, the archivist preserves materials and sets the rules for their collection, weeding out series of documents that do not stand up to appraisal criteria. Using the tenets of his profession, the archivist works to gather documentation that illuminates particular times, places, and persons who shape events and culture.

> *Your job is not about storing and sorting information. It is about appraising and keeping records of history-making events and the acts spoken by history-makers, and doing that in a way*

---

84. Hackman and Warnow-Blewett quoting the Society of American Archivists Task Force on Goals and Priorities, 14.

> *that allows you to be effective partners for those history-makers in their remembering of the past. Such a story will make clear that your job is not to compete with computers, software, and emerging computer networks in the categorization, storage, and retrieval of data. Santa Ana [sic] did not say those who could not retrieve the information were condemned to be unhappy or to produce more of the same information. He said those who could not re-member — i.e., assemble an effective interpretation of the past — would repeat that past.*[85]

But how does a professional know the appropriate ways to build a collection that will properly reflect society? Once a niche has been defined for a repository's collecting practices, how does one focus on the nitty-gritty of choosing one group of records over another? Appraisal is the act of constructing a collection by choosing the resources that are assessed to meet the repository's criteria for collection development. Over the past one hundred years, the archives profession has grappled with appraisal issues and has developed its theories to assist us with formulating decisions about what to keep and what to discard or reject. These theories were devised to accommodate the massive growth of recorded information and changes in ideas about who should be included when we document history. As we approached and entered the twenty-first century, archival thought evolved to be all-inclusive and collaborative.

---

85. Chauncey Bell, *Organizational Change: What Is It and What Does It Mean for Records Professionals* (keynote address to National Association of Government Archives and Record Administrators, Sacramento, California, 1997), available at http://www.mybestdocs.com/. Antonio López de Santa Anna was a nineteenth-century Mexican president and general and is best known for defeating Texans at the Battle of the Alamo in 1836.

In 1922, Hilary Jenkinson proposed an early appraisal theory in his *Manual of Archival Appraisal*. His theory established creator value, stating that records are important as by-products of human activity and should be maintained without tampering. Archivists were not partners in the documentation process, but were keepers of the past who kept what historians told them was important. The record creator was recognized as the authority in determining the importance of his records because he was so closely tied intellectually and emotionally to them. According to Jenkinson's theory, the person managing what is and is not added to a collection would not be the same person who takes care of the records and understands the overall scope of a collection. This was soon seen as a problem by other archives theorists.

Once people realized the inability of the creator of documents to remain impartial about them, they looked to archivists to fill the role as objective keepers and developers of the documentary record. Archivists must make difficult decisions to retain only those resources that add value to the historical memory. A creator may think that his records are important, but only one who is well versed in related collections and who has an understanding of the role a collection plays in the overall documentation of a subject or activity can properly appraise materials.

In 1956, Theodore Schellenberg introduced the idea of "user value."[86] This proposed that if someone could use the records for any reason, then it has value. Schellenberg defined values as *primary* and *secondary*. The primary value for an institutional record is the reason for which it was created, including administrative, legal, and fiscal uses.

---

86. Theodore Schellenberg, "The Appraisal of Modern Public Records," National Archives Bulletin 8: National Archives and Records Service, 1956. Reprinted in Ed. Maygene F. Daniels and Timothy Walch, *A Modern Archives Reader: Basic Readings on Archival Theory and Practice* (Washington D.C. National Archives and Records Service, 1984), 57–70.

Personal papers, such as diaries and letters, have a primary social use. The secondary value of a record is its value to outsiders, such as researchers, and this value is often recognized after the record is no longer needed to fulfill its primary purpose.

Secondary value is defined as evidential or informational. Evidential value provides verification of an organization's activities through financial records and similar types of substantiating papers. Informational value includes any insight that a document provides, even if it wasn't created specifically to provide that knowledge. For example, census records are used for many purposes beyond their primary purpose and tell us a lot about society. According to Schellenberg, records cast light upon the functioning of the administrative body, describe the history of the administrative body, and meet scholarly needs for information in general.

Schellenberg's appraisal theories had a great impact on the way many archivists viewed themselves. His work suggested that the creator determined the primary value of the record and the archivist determined the secondary value. This opened the door for the archivist to become an appraiser of records rather than just a caretaker.

However, Schellenberg also believed that if a researcher can use any record, then it has value, making it difficult for the archivist to reject any collections at all. This idea led many to haphazardly collect everything that came across their paths rather than instituting well-planned collection development policies to focus collections and to ensure that history was adequately documented. Archivists soon learned that we must not respond to the whims of researchers or "the vogue of the academic marketplace."[87] According to archivist Gerald Ham, "Most researchers are

---

87. Gerald Ham, "The Archival Edge," *The American Archivist* 38 (Jan. 1975): 8.

caught in their own concerns and do not worry about all the history that needs to be written; yet in terms of documentary preservation this is precisely what the archivist must do. Small wonder, then, that archival holdings [based on the creator theory or on researchers' desires] too often reflected narrow research interest rather than the broad spectrum of human experience. If we cannot transcend these obstacles, then the archivist will remain at best nothing more than a weathervane moved by the changing winds of historiography."[88]

The Schellenberg appraisal theory also falls short for modern archives due to the vast amount of written, oral, and visual information produced every day in contemporary society. When Schellenberg was writing, recorded information was much less prolific. Today's archives must take into account the massive records generated by computers. According to Ham, "With records increasing at an exponential rate, it is utopian to believe that society could ever afford the resources for us to preserve everything of possible value; for it to do so would be irresponsible."[89] Ham also points out that while the volume of information has increased, its quality has decreased due to the ease with which it is created. It is therefore important for the archivist to serve as an appraiser, retaining only that which serves to enhance the documentary record.

Schellenberg's prime contribution to modern thinking was his advancement of the idea of a record's life cycle. He proclaimed that an archivist should follow the life of the records from their creation to their disposition. He purported that archives and records management go hand-in-hand. The records management field focuses on active records, while Archives focus on records to be kept for

---

88. Ham, 8.
89. Ham, 9

posterity past their active lives. The idea of the record life cycle is important to the archivist who is trying to understand the full scope of collections. It was once thought that archivists should only care for records once their "useful" active life was over, but Schellenberg encouraged archivists to understand what was being created so they could tag it for the Archives before it had a chance to disappear through disposition or was lost and forgotten among other papers. In contemporary society it is especially important to track institutional collections and computerized records that can disappear in a flash.[90]

In the mid- and late twentieth century, archivists began theorizing that record collecting should extend beyond evaluating the records themselves to evaluating society and how records should and did reflect trends in culture. It was not until this point, archivist Hans Booms contended, that historians considered it "significant that, besides the workings of chance, the ways in which archivists design, mould, and shape the documentary record might also have an effect on the 'historical picture.'"[91]

In the 1980s, Helen Samuels furthered the European idea of looking beyond what is in your immediate collection to examine the full scope of produced records. Her community documentation strategy encouraged archivists to determine what needs to be created to record

---

90. In the United States, David Bearman's writings have introduced a new paradigm to care for and appraise records in his writings "Archival Methods" (Pittsburgh, Archives & Museum Informatics, 1989) and "Archival Strategies" (*The American Archivist*, vol. 58, 1994, 374–407). His views are mirrored by the Australian "Records Continuum Model." These methods encourage the collaborative "integration of recordkeeping and archiving processes," according to Professor Sue McKemmish, and discourage the distinct separation of a record's life stages. This theory is especially important to many working with electronic records, who seek to define better ways to capture and preserve important digital documents from their inception. See Sue McKemmish, "Yesterday, Today and Tomorrow: A Continuum of Responsibility," Proceedings of the Records Management Association of Australia 14th National Convention, 15–17 (Sept 1997), and RMAA Perth and Xiaomi An, "An Integrated Approach to Records Management," *The Information Management Journal* (July/August 2003): 24–30.
91. Booms, 81.

undocumented or under-documented events, while gathering existing records that best reflect society's activities.[92] Samuels encouraged multidisciplinary groups to work together and focus collecting strategies in different areas. Sharing the burden of appraisal, the archivist relies on the expertise of those in numerous fields to assist in deciding what records are necessary to enhance the documentary record. A key element of Samuels's strategy is that more effort is spent in planning a collection strategy than in appraising records after they have arrived at the archives.

Using the documentation strategy, the archivist is a facilitator who encourages others to use their knowledge of their fields to help decide what documentation is necessary to properly preserve and record knowledge about culture. The archivist is the overseer who may serve final judgment over what should be saved and what should be discarded, but she uses the expertise of others to help her make decisions about what will enhance the documentary record. Samuels recognized that the archivist could not be an expert in all areas of scholarly research and social knowledge, but the archivist must have the skills to learn from the experts, filter the experts' biases, and use other theories of archival appraisal to make ultimate decisions about collection development. Archivists and others who care for records in a professional manner "are often the ones who understand most about documents as we ponder over their order and content, trying to remain sensitive to as many implications as we can.... It is this awareness of documents and the nature of their relationship to both past and present which has grown from our constant exposure to

---

[92] Helen Samuels. "Who Controls the Past," *The American Archivist.* 49. 2 (Spring 1986.)

records prior to and after their structuring in our archives."[93]

Samuels's work also brought the idea of collaborative collecting into the limelight. Archivists were realizing that the concept of a collection should not end at their institution's doors and that an Archives is not a self-contained entity. Rather, archivists should work together with colleagues and field specialists on collecting plans to ensure that there are no gaps in the documentary record. Plans should be formulated to ensure that the documentation of a specific issue or event is complete. The strategy for documentation is ongoing, requiring institutions to place cooperation and collaboration as one of their primary administrative tasks for continued successful operation. Cooperation should be as valued as processing collections or providing reference services to ensure such success.

Around the same time that Samuels formulated her theory, Terry Cook promoted the idea of functional appraisal, addressing how archives reflect values, trends, and functions in society as determined by the archivist, perhaps with advice from others. Cook talked about the "total archives" and "macro-appraisal" approach used in Canada, which emphasizes the need for institutional archivists to ensure that saving recorded evidence of an organization's activities remains at the forefront of his responsibilities. Based on earlier work by Gerald Ham, Cook's ideas also emphasized "the cultural role of archives as preservers of societal memory and historical identity," allowing archives to place emphasis on the whole of the documentary record rather than giving one type of record

---

93. Hugh Taylor, "Clio in the Raw: Archival Materials and the Teaching of History," *The American Archivist* (July/October 1972): 329.

more import than another.[94] This approach overlapped with Samuels's documentation theory and paralleled her later writings on "institutional functional analysis" by describing the need for institutional archivists to examine the evidential record within their own institutions based on a thorough understanding of the functioning of their own organization.[95] These archivists could then properly participate in larger community documentation projects that took place outside of, but also involved, their organizations. According to Cook, "Appraisal is a work of careful analysis and of archival, diplomatic, and historical scholarship, not a mere procedure or process. Applying guidelines or checklists in the appraisal process, as well as developing broader acquisition strategies, only works if such application is based on a rich understanding by the archivist of the history of the records creator, its official functions and legal mandates, its internal organizational structure, its decision-making processes, its records-creating procedures, and the changes in all these over time, as well as a similar understanding of the often subtle characteristics of the records themselves."[96]

Archival theories should be used to manage collections individually and collaboratively. Archivists must think about their repository's users, the intention of the record creator, society, and the records themselves to establish efficient and useful collections. It is not an easy process, nor is it a strict science. It is the contemporary archivist's goal to gather the records of society and collect materials that produce "a narrative in which all participants

---

94. Terry Cook, "What Is Past Is Prologue: A History of Archival Ideas Since 1898, and the Future Paradigm Shift," *Archivaria* 43 (Spring 97); text available at http://www.mybestdocs.com/cookt-pastprologue-ar43fnl.htm.
95. Helen Samuels, *Varsity Letters: Documenting Modern Colleges and Universities* (Chicago: Society of American Archivists, 1992).
96. Cook, *The Archival Appraisal of Records Containing Personal Information: A RAMP Study with Guidelines.*

[of society] can find themselves, with perspectives determined by personal histories and the values they uphold. This is the process of history."[97] It is difficult to remove our own biases from the process of collection development. It is virtually impossible for the archivist to overcome inserting, to some degree, her personal values from the collecting process. But we must consider our values harmonized with the values of others, combined with the application of archival theory and what we can realistically achieve, to enact appropriate appraisal decisions and achieve the most balanced collections possible.

97. Archibald, 63.

**Some Key Concepts in the Development of Appraisal Theory**

**1922**

Englishman Sir Hilary Jenkinson proposes that those who create records are the best prepared to evaluate their value and ascertain their authenticity.

**1944**

Illinois state archivist Margaret Cross Norton and Philip C. Brooks of the National Archives propose that there is a need for a better way to select the records we preserve. They introduce the idea of a record's life cycle.

**1956**

Theodore R. Schellenberg develops the idea of a record's life cycle and introduces the concepts that lead people to call him "the father of appraisal theory in the United States." While working for the National Archives, Schellenberg creates the idea that records have primary and secondary values. The primary value, judged by the record creator, relates to why the record was made. The secondary (or informational) value, judged by an archivist, considers a document's potential uses after it has served its primary purpose.

**1975**

Wisconsin's state archivist Gerald Ham states that appraisal is an archivist's most important and challenging task and that we need to do it better. He and other archivists want to develop an historical record that reflects society and properly considers ever-changing record practices.

**1980s**

MIT archivist Helen Samuels presents the documentation strategy. The theory encourages archivists to work collaboratively to make decisions about what to keep to enhance the documentary record.

Working at the National Archives of Canada, Terry Cook elaborates on the idea of evaluating archives based on how they reflect society. Called macro-appraisal, his theory focuses on the functions of institutions.

This list identifies some key thoughts related to archival appraisal. There are many other archivists who have contributed to the theory and have helped those above create the path for better selection of materials for preservation in Archives.

Records serve as evidence of their creators' actions and society's functions and should be valued on multiple levels by diverse groups for their authenticity, the information they provide, and their reflection of society.

## Writing the Mission Statement

A mission statement is a declaration of purpose that explains the role of an organization and whom it serves. It is an important tool that formalizes and establishes a tone for the functioning of a repository. The mission statement for an institution should reflect its reasons for acquiring and providing access to materials. It should include a summary description of what the organization collects. A mission statement should be succinct. It is a general statement out of which all the administrative documents created by an institution must grow. The mission of the cultural heritage organization is the foundation upon which its collections are based. A well-articulated mission precedes the writing of the collection development policy and should be included in that policy. "As those with actual experience in their preparation can testify, the formulation of well-considered collections management policy involves far more than simply thinking through the procedures to be followed with respect to owned or borrowed collections. It also involves a thorough articulation of the museum's fundamental purpose and, above all, an analysis of the relationship of its owned collections to that purpose."[98]

A mission statement guides collecting and must be considered when organizations collaborate to fully document their communities. It is another tool that helps an organization find its documentation niche. Effective collaborating repositories have missions that reflect a shared sense of purpose with the safeguarding of historical resources as a core function. When properly written, a

---

98. Ed. Stephen E. Weil, *A Deaccession Reader*, (Washington, D.C.: American Association of Museums, 1997), 4.

mission will reflect the important role that archives play in a cultural heritage repository's activities.

Primarily, the collection development policy will reflect the principles to which the mission statement prescribes. According to David Carr, "The museum's statement of mission is a public expression of promise; therefore, it is an obligation under the care of administrators, trustees, employees, and volunteers. An articulate mission makes clear that all of the museum's work is done in the presence of an obligation to adhere to its aims; therefore, the first criterion of ethical practice is the prominent embodiment of mission in even the smallest of the museum's plans and activities."[99] The mission should define what the organization does, how it does it, and for whom. When properly written, the mission statement defines a clear path for policies and procedure. The mission should be understandable, concise, and all-encompassing. It should distinguish the institution it represents from other similar organizations. When necessary, the revision of a mission should aim to clarify it rather than changing the core concepts that are important to the institution. These core values should only be changed if major revisions to the institution itself take place, such as a merger.

The core elements of a mission statement include:

- A description of the organization's purpose in terms of what it collects and what activities it conducts
- A discussion of the role the organization plays in the community and the collecting world based on its defined purpose
- An explanation of the audience the institution serves defined by their professions, common interests, similar

99. David Carr, *The Promise of Cultural Institutions* (Walnut Creek, MD: AltaMira Press, 2003), 119.

concerns, geographic locale, age, gender, ethnicity, or other shared traits

The mission statement supports the collection development policy by providing a guide of what is important to the institution. It provides a general framework under which all collection development, appraisal policies, and decisions should be made. During the writing or rewriting of the collections policy, the writers should ensure that the elements of the policy reflect the principles of the mission, fitting collecting goals firmly within the strictures of the organization's overall purpose. The mission statement should precisely define the people, areas, and activities the repository documents. A very general mission statement can easily accommodate any collecting parameters an institution desires. However, too general a statement does not help the collecting focus of the institution. A good mission statement will strike a balance between ambiguity and specificity, but it must provide strong guidelines for decision-making, or the policies that grow from it will not have a solid foundation.

The mission statement should define an institution's core purpose and include all of the elements that are important and permanent to the institution. In times of peril, when an institution may seek to cut back programs and activities, the mission serves to define the institution's priorities. When collections are not defined in the mission, when records are not even mentioned, it is much easier for an institution to make decisions to reduce funding for archives or place less emphasis on their importance than when the collections are defined in print as valuable to the overall purpose of the institution. When a mission statement lists the particular collections it seeks, collecting goals are tied to the core of the institution's purpose and are taken seriously.

The mission statement should serve as a public relations tool. "Call it a PR statement if you will, but have a simple, easy-to-remember and repeat statement that your board members, staff, and volunteers can effectively use to lobby on behalf of your organization."[100] A clear statement will enable an institution to run more effectively by facilitating its communication of function and will help it attract donors, researchers, and collaborators who support this purpose. An effective mission statement will allow outsiders to better understand an institution and to recognize the professionalism in how it is run, making them more willing to support all of its activities.

To this end, those with experience writing mission statements say that the best ones are short and succinct — no more than a paragraph long. When used as a PR tool, the mission should be short enough to recite in an elevator. However, it is important to make sure the mission is also comprehensive, which may entail expanding on an original general statement, writing objectives, and/or including a vision statement. These items should provide more detailed information about the mission. They may expand on the elements of collections and activities of an organization, specifying roles and how activities are managed. Objectives help direct specific functions but should not introduce new concepts that were not alluded to in the mission itself.

If an establishment does not solely function as an archival repository, it can create a mission statement specifically for its archives and should incorporate the role of the archives into the organization's primary mission statement. The mission or missions should clearly define the purpose of the archival collection and its relationship to the parent institution. The purpose of the Archives should

---

100. The Evergreen State Society, "What Should Our Mission Statement Say?" (Seattle, Washington: Internet Nonprofit Center, 2003): http://www.nonprofits.org/npofaq/03/21.html.

grow from that of the parent institution and cement its significance to the institution's overall goals.

The mission statement and documents that spring from it should be reviewed and approved by the institution's administration so they receive the proper authority. Better yet, all members of the institution, from the board to the curator, should participate in the writing of such documents to ensure broad-based empathy and support for the organization's functioning and affirmation of the institution's sense of self. Specifically, the support of the institution's overall governing body is essential to the success of collection development. It is important to seek this approval before it is needed. If policies are challenged, it is easier to defend them when people start in agreement of a vision. When challenges occur from outside, those overseeing the institutions who back the clearly defined (and printed) policies and procedures are formidable advocates of specific programs. A qualified attorney should review formal policies to ensure that they conform to legal requirements to further strengthen the imperative of the written documents.

A separate mission statement can be written to support a multi-institutional collaborative effort. "Well-crafted mission statements describe the purpose of the collaborative venture, clarify why participants have become involved and communicate to local constituents and funding agents."[101] The collaborative mission statement should discuss the role of each institution within the collaborative, using each individual institutional mission statement as a supportive document for the creation of a broader view.[102]

---

101. James Burgett, John Haar, and Linda L Phillips, *Collaborative Collection Development: A Practical Guide for Your Library* (Chicago: American Library Association, 2004), 89.
102. See Alexandra Yarrow, Barbara Clubb, and Jennifer-Lynn Draper, "Public Libraries, Archives and Museums: Trends in Collaboration and Cooperation," IFLA

The mission statement should be prominent and easily accessible to staff and the public. Staff should be well-versed with the mission so that they are all working with a clear and universally accepted vision for operations. The mission statement should be included in brochures introducing the institution and on the repository's Web site, providing all interested parties with a clear comprehension of the scope of the cultural heritage institution's practices and purpose.

The following sample mission statements come from three diverse historical societies. The institutions reflect dissimilar areas of the country and were founded in diverse eras. Each institution focuses its role on the culture of its locale, continually refining mission statements as time progresses and society evolves. Chosen to illustrate how the general diverse collecting nature of historical societies can be characterized, these institutions have successfully defined their broad sights in short statements that help give clarity and focus to their intentions.

---

Professional Reports, no. 108 (International Federation of Library Associations and Institutions, 2008): 19–20. The collaborative mission statements of ABM-centrum in Sweden and Bibliothèque et Archives nationales du Québec (BAnQ) in Montreal, Canada, that they include serve as good examples for groups.

---

**Sample Mission Statement 1**
**Wildwood Historical Society, Missouri**

Wildwood, Missouri, has a population of approximately 35,000 residents and is located about 30 miles outside of St. Louis. Founded in 1995, Wildwood is one of Missouri's newest cities and is the state's third largest in area. The Wildwood Historical Society was founded in 1999 and operates with the help of almost fifty volunteers dedicated to helping preserve the area's heritage. The historical society once accepted all donations, but with the purchase of a larger space, it desires to better focus collecting efforts. Over the past fifteen years, it has learned how quickly new collections can fill a storage area. The institution serves as the only formal collecting cultural heritage repository in the city and seeks to preserve as much of the story of its community as it can. The historical society's original mission statement is broad and will soon be revised by members trying to ensure that the items that best illustrate the heritage and unique qualities of the region are retained.

The original mission outlines the types of materials the institution collects and its purpose for collecting. It discusses the additional activities of the historical society that grow from collecting efforts. It also briefly identifies the society's audience. The mission can be strengthened by better defining who might be interested in the repository's collections by explaining the periods reflected in its holdings and by identifying how Wildwood's history is reflected in those eras.

The historical society's mission supports its collections policy. Both the mission and collecting efforts will be reexamined in coordination with its move. This new historical society in this newly incorporated locale is purposefully reevaluating volunteers' earliest assumptions about the growth of their institution and is redirecting future documentation efforts accordingly. The historical society would also do well to seek out collaborative partners in neighboring communities that may have overlapping collections. These early efforts at putting professional management strategies in place will help the institution establish a firm identity in the collecting community.

The Wildwood Historical Society's mission:

The purpose of the Wildwood Historical Society is to discover, memorialize, and disseminate the prehistory and history of the City of Wildwood, Missouri, by:
1. Searching for and procuring written and photographic documentation (including, but not limited to, personal writings or photographs, newspaper articles, relics, memorabilia, and/or other similar documents, items, or objects relating to the history and prehistory of Wildwood.
2. Preserving, displaying, and making available to the public these documents, items, and objects by placing them in a museum/library/research center and in exhibits strategically located throughout Wildwood.
3. Identifying and helping to maintain and preserve historic and prehistoric homes, buildings, and/or other structures and/or sites.
4. Maintaining an active outreach and education program for historical society members and the general public.
5. Accepting donations of money, real property, and/or other property as appropriate to accomplish the above.

http://www.wildwoodhistoricalsociety.org/about.html

---

---

**Sample Mission Statement 2**
**Lyon County Historical Society, Kansas**

Lyon County, Kansas, was established in 1858 and currently maintains a population of approximately 36,000 people. It is also the home of the Lyon County Historical Society, which was founded in 1937. The organization is the only repository in the area and focuses on an educational purpose that promotes the heritage of the region. It builds its collections to support this instructive function, carefully ensuring that materials fit within the historical society's scope. The historical society seeks collections relevant to the local history of Lyon County.

The management of the Lyon County Historical Society is under the direction of one full-time employee and five part-time employees. The organization recently instituted and is in the process of implementing a strategic plan to further its goals. A priority within the plan was the rewriting of a mission statement to better define the institution's purpose. As a result, the new mission statement reflects standard museum goals to support education, research, preservation, exhibition, and interpretation of both artifacts and archives. The specific citing of these functions ties them directly to the organization's identity, ensuring their importance is recognized and their incorporation into the historical society's day-to-day activities is upheld. The mission statement also refers to the "unique identity of Lyon County," requiring individuals to think about their cultural heritage and to reflect on what makes the area distinctive. Upon this simple statement of purpose, the standards of museum management are supported and the functions of the repository grow.

The Lyon County Historical Society has established a Web site, and its Friends group has established a presence on Facebook that allows it to convey its mission and better communicate with its intended audience. Many museums are working hard to use Web 2.0 applications to create Web sites, create Facebook pages, and use Twitter. They are experimenting with how the Internet can benefit their institutions. Should this tool become a more integral part of the Lyon County Historical Society's outreach efforts, and if it is used more often to generate educational discussion, it would benefit the organization to include its online presence in its mission.[103]

The Lyon County Historical Society's mission:

The mission of the Lyon County Museum and Historical Society is to provide education and research, and to promote the appreciation of our unique heritage through the preservation, exhibition, and interpretation of artifacts and archival material representing the history of Lyon County, Kansas.

http://www.lyoncountymuseum.org

---

103. See the Lyon County Historical Society Facebook page at http://bit.ly/8Zqt48.

**Sample Mission Statement 3**
**Groton Historical Society Museum, Massachusetts**

Groton, Massachusetts, was founded in 1655 and currently is a Boston bedroom community with a population of about 10,000 residents. Located in the house of George S. Boutwell (who served as governor of the Commonwealth for two terms [1851–1853] and as Secretary of the Treasury under President Ulysses S. Grant), the Groton Historical Society Museum was incorporated in 1894. The institution works to broadly collect resources of varied media highlighting Groton's history. The historical society is the only formal collecting repository in town gathering personal papers and artifacts with a Groton connection. Guided by a wide-ranging mission statement to accomplish the task of broad collecting, the institution seeks to preserve materials and ensure that its collections are actively used by patrons.

The historical society's mission statement focuses on three functions. The first part addresses the collections themselves, defining collecting, preservation, and exhibit purposes and a general framework for the types of materials to be housed in the repository. The second part discusses the historical society as a communal organization that invites those with an interest in history to see it as a place for sharing those interests. The third part of the mission discusses a focus on outreach to increase interest in local history through historical society activities.

The historical society takes its outreach and fraternal role as seriously as its collecting role, and this is boosted by the mention of those two elements in the mission statement. The organization has worked hard to give people a place to gather to learn about history, trying to emphasize that it is not just a repository "filled with old things," but a place where history can come to life through hands-on examination of materials and through programs that try to focus on Groton society.

Within the collections policy, the Groton Historical Society Museum's mission statement is preceded by an introduction that states, "The Groton Historical Society was incorporated in 1894 as an institution dedicated to preserving and recording the history of Groton, Massachusetts. For over 100 years the Society has been actively collecting artifacts relating to Groton and its people and has displayed these artifacts in our museum located in the home of the youngest Massachusetts Governor, George S. Boutwell." The historical society's presence in this historic home gives it a unique dimension that is not addressed in the following mission. The role of the house within the historical society's mission has been considered through its history. Should the institution decide to more actively promote the Boutwell story and its connection to it, this can be incorporated as a fourth component of the mission statement: to better communicate its value to the historical society and to its community.

From its inception through the present, the historical society has refined its purpose to reflect changes in culture. At the turn of the twentieth century, the organization's bylaws stated, "The object of the Society shall be to collect and preserve manuscripts, printed books, pamphlets, historical facts, biographical anecdotes, and historical relics, and to stimulate research into local history, especially of the towns included within the original limits of Groton." By the mid-twentieth century, the purpose sought to reflect a growing desire to get people interested in local history work. The Groton Historical Society's 1950 bylaws state, “The object of the Society shall be the furtherance of interest in the study of local history and stimulation of collecting and preserving printed and manuscript matter; also articles of historical and antiquarian interest, especially of the towns included in the original limits of Groton.” The current mission reflects modern society’s desire to have its institutions reach out to the public in multifaceted ways to encourage an appreciation of cultural heritage and the local institution that supports it.

The Groton Historical Society’s mission:

The Mission of the Groton Historical Society is to collect, preserve, and display objects, records, and folklore of historic significance from Groton’s past and to maintain a museum for these artifacts and records according to current museum standards. It also provides an organization for those residents interested in preserving and maintaining the local history of Groton and to familiarize a wider community of citizens with Groton’s history and increase interest in local history and tradition through exhibits, educational programs, publications, and historical records.

http://www.grotonhistoricalsociety.org

---

## Writing the Collection Development Policy

As a repository that keeps archival documents, the most specific tool an organization will create to control collections is a collection development policy.[104] This policy sharpens the focus of a collection, helps when dealing with donors, assists in handling unwanted material, and facilitates coordination, cooperation, and collaboration. A collection development policy for records in one's care should grow from the repository's mission. "The task [of writing the policy] should be viewed as an opportunity to codify and perhaps clarify the goals of the museum and the methods used to achieve these goals, and to assure that there are effective procedures for periodic evaluation."[105]

The policy must be viewed as a guide for voicing our intentions and setting us on a path for focused collecting. In addition to directing collecting practices, a policy helps demonstrate that collection development is thoughtful and properly managed. "The collecting policy must be based on the needs of users, on other repositories' collecting goals, on budget allocations, and on complimentary and secondary research materials."[106] It allows everyone to understand the purpose of the collections and to work to achieve common goals. The creation of a collection development policy is an important management step that will not only save time in the long

---

104. The archives planning document we call the "collection development policy" is referred to by alternate titles cross-professionally and within the field. It may also commonly be known as a collection management policy, collections policy, collecting policy, or a collection plan.
105. Marie C. Malaro, "Collections Management Policies," *Museum News* (November/December 1979): 59.
106. Faye Phillips, "Developing Collection Development Policies for Manuscript Repositories," *The American Archivist* 47.1 (Winter 1984): 33.

run and help an institution to be more organized and insightful about its collection management strategies, but it will also allow the institution to better understand the ways that its holdings help and can be used by the public. Despite these benefits, less than 40 percent of archival repositories had a collection development policy when the Council of State Archivists last surveyed United States repositories relative to this issue.[107]

Time, staff, and funding can greatly influence the priority an institution attaches to creating formal written policies. The writing of the policy is time-consuming and should involve people from multiple ranks within the institution. Efforts to collaborate in this way internally, similar to efforts to collaborate with outside institutions, can be challenging. However, well-written policies provide an overarching framework that makes all future tasks easier to accomplish and less time-consuming. A good administrative base created through the development of thoughtful managerial tools helps a repository appear and feel more organized, which will help it garner outside support for additional donations, human resources, and funding. It is well worth the effort to create such a policy. It is a critical component for the professionalism of any cultural heritage institution.

"How can archivists expect others to respect their repository's collection development policy when they themselves treat it as an occasional tool rather than an integral part of the repository?"[108] Archivists should use a collection development policy every day for public relations and collection management decisions. The policy should serve as the main guide for the growth of

---

107. Victoria Irons Walch, comp., *Where History Begins: A Report on Historical Records Repositories in the United States* (Council of State Historical Records Coordinators, May 1998): 22.
108. Sauer, 325.

collections. It should be one of the main instruments for explaining an organization's purpose to the public. Combined with donor forms, the collection development policy should clearly state an institution's responsibilities to a donor, including what the donor can expect in terms of processing, use, and maintenance of the materials he is offering.

If archives management is not the main goal of an institution, the organization should write a policy that incorporates the spectrum of materials it collects. The role of archives in an institution should be just one piece of a broader collections policy in a repository that collects diverse resources. The writer of the plan must discuss the role each type of material plays within the overall collecting scheme — describing materials as items to be displayed, to be referred to as supporting documents for alternate collections, or to serve as primary source materials for patron research. Organizations should aim to define all the materials they collect and how they relate. The collections fit together like a puzzle, with each type of material relating to the institution's mission and supporting the others as informational resources and cultural treasures. If the main role of collecting archives is to support an institution's other collections, this must be acknowledged. On a broader level, the collection development policy must cite the mission of the institution and explain how each collection format supports the organization's mission.

According to the American Association of Museums, one-fourth of museums that have had accreditation tabled have problems with collection stewardship, including low levels of documentation and poor focus, in addition to poor preservation and planning practices.[109] The care and collection development of

---

109. Ed. James B. Gardner and Elizabeth E. Merritt, *The AAM Guide to Collections Planning* (Washington, D.C.: American Association of Museums, 2004), 1.

records in tandem with care of other resources in a museum helps the institution think about and develop its sense of identity, sense of purpose, and direction. Professional associations recognize that the establishment of a collections policy creates a foundation for an organization's success. The policy defines the institution's responsibilities to the collection itself and to the public it serves.

A comprehensive collection development plan should include basic information describing the collections and how they are managed.[110] The document can be long and include information about outreach, access, processing, and donations. However, some repositories choose to place procedure information in separate administrative tools and do not duplicate these elements in the collection development policy itself. The administrative document should conform to the institution's culture, including components that properly define the institution's role, which are articulated through a thoughtful planning process. Formatting and specific content of collecting plans may differ among policies to suit institutional culture, but all should clearly define the scope of the collections and proffer information about the future of collection development.

As a guide for collection growth, the collection policy should be broad yet specific, requiring some interpretation to guarantee some flexibility. It is not a rigid template for collecting, but a guide for best practices. Archival collecting is not an exact science, and we must use our best-informed judgment to make logical and ethical decisions. Many archivists are concerned that a collection development policy will limit what their institutions can collect. Good collection planning necessarily sets limits to create clearly understandable guidelines, yet it considers all

---

110. For more detailed information about the parts of a collection development policy, see Phillips, 39–42.

possible future acquisitions. The document is written so anything that may interest an institution for a logical reason can fit within its scope. "The policy should be flexible enough to permit prudent ad hoc decisions concerning unusual opportunities that may arise."[111]

Sometimes collections out of the scope of our policies are accepted to prevent their destruction, to cement a relationship with a valuable donor, or to develop an even stronger collection with more leverage. When we consider going against our guide for collecting, we should do it with a clear understanding of where it will lead us, how it will change our focus, and how it changes our relationship with our collaborative institutions. Your first choice should be to refer an unsuitable collection elsewhere. If you find it desirable to take in a collection outside the scope of an institution's collections policy, you must reexamine the written policy and revise it to explain the housing of the new material in the facility, making sure to consider if the collection does appropriately fall within the institution's larger mission. In other words, taking in a collection outside of our written collection scope must be carefully considered. It should be done only in extreme circumstances when we find it fitting to change the previous direction of our collecting strategy.

Alternately, a well-written collection development policy can sometimes be used to justify accepting a collection that you might not normally consider. When you do the legwork necessary to create a collection development policy, you are more familiar with an institution's holdings and have a better understanding of the breadth of the archives. An archivist may notice a connection between a potential donation and existing collections that otherwise may have gone unobserved. A

---

111. Malaro, 59.

collection development policy can validate the types of materials an institution accepts, whether you desire controversial collections to provide a balanced view on a subject or you accept a donation that will provide some exposure for an underutilized collection already within an institution's holdings.

To explain our purpose to the public, repositories must provide clear distinctions between their collections and others. Defining a focus for your collecting allows researchers to better understand where to find the materials they need. In addition to its community function, the documentation plan, discussed earlier, helps institutions develop or rewrite their own policies while taking into account a more global perspective. A main component of community documentation is the review of in-house collecting and the writing/revising of an individual institution's collection development plans. Returning to your own planning documents after working in a collaborative group allows you to incorporate a more comprehensive viewpoint within your institution. Distinctive collections with clear goals and missions allow users to better understand the types of materials that are available, how those materials should be used, how to better identify the materials they need, and how to articulate those needs to collection caretakers.

When dealing with donors, a clear collection development policy helps you actively seek collections, turn down inappropriate donations, properly allocate funds for unique materials that don't duplicate those in other repositories, and work in a planned direction, rather than appraising individual collections solely on a case-by-case basis. Active collecting, conforming to both the repository's mission and collection development policy, will make the repository stronger through greater visibility and increased understanding of the institution's holdings.

For the growth of the archives collection, archivists should also use the collection development policy to target records that are important to keep for posterity as they are created, rather than trying to track them down years later. This makes it easier to reach out and find appropriate records, garner community support, show the vitality of your organization, and collect materials most meaningful to documentation efforts. Information about active records should be included within the collection development policy. Targeting records for collection as they are created helps ensure that they will be properly cared for throughout their lifetime. An archives repository should reach out to record keepers in their town (including businesses, associations, and private individuals) to learn about the types of materials they create prior to the writing of the collection policy. Cultural heritage institutions must aim to raise awareness about which records that individuals and institutions create are important to the community as a whole and are appropriate for an archival facility once their functional lives have ended. To further alert the public to its collecting needs, a repository may include a "wish list" within the collections policy to highlight those records that are missing from the documentary record and may be in private hands.

A reasonable time frame for processing collections may be included in a collection development policy. It must take into account staffing and budgetary levels and consider what an institution can reasonably process. A repository must not collect more than it can handle. Keeping up to date with the work at hand makes a repository appear more professional and more attractive to outsiders, such as potential volunteers. A pile of unprocessed collections makes the research institution appear disorganized. It can be a source of irritation for donors who expect to see their collections in use within a reasonable time after they are transferred to a repository. It also can be a source of low morale for staff who can feel overwhelmed as they are continually trying to reduce the number of unprocessed collections. Unprocessed collections that sit in Archives for years are useless to the Archives and to their patrons.[112] The archivist is responsible for processing the collection in a reasonable amount of time so that the arrangement and the informational value are preserved for every potential user.

Good working relationships with partner institutions should be reaffirmed by offering records that would otherwise be backlogged to other appropriate facilities. Careful use of the collection development policy and appraisal theories prevents accumulation of unprocessed collections and ensures that an institution is maintaining collections that are most important to its direct mission. An institution may choose to offer to collaborative organizations overflow collections that are only peripheral to the vision of an overwhelmed repository.

Through the development and use of the guidelines in collecting policies, an institution can more easily work together with others to achieve the ideal comprehensive documentation of local history described earlier. The writing of individual collecting policies for repositories assists cooperation and collaboration by enabling institutions to fill a specific documentation gap and helping them to eliminate competition among collecting partners. Without a policy for collecting, an institution will try to collect in too broad an area, leaving gaps in their own collections and in the documentary record. The collection policy is the primary tool that allows us to identify our

---

112. Researchers should not be allowed to use unprocessed collections because of the associated risks to materials, including the possible loss of original arrangement and preservation issues. There is also a risk of harm when an archivist is unaware of the scope of a collection because it has not yet been processed, leaving it open to theft and mishandling.

niche in a wide network of similar collecting institutions. "Collection Management focuses on the need to build coherent collections and to make the process as consistent, cost effective, and user-beneficial as possible. To meet these goals, selection should be proactive; that is, acquisitions should be actively chosen and not merely passively accepted. Selection should recognize the need for increased specialization. Few archives or libraries can afford to sustain comprehensive collections in a number of subjects."[113]

Repositories should also consider, and research, what organizations outside of the region are collecting to hone their own focus. The National Union Catalog of Manuscript Collections is a good starting source to determine what others are collecting related to a particular subject.[114] Awareness of other repositories with similar focus will also later allow you to guide donors to more appropriate facilities, assist researchers, and develop mutually beneficial cooperative programs with other cultural institutions inside and outside of your region.

Institutional Archives, which collect and care for records generated by their parent organization, may create a records management plan in lieu of a collections policy. The plan discusses which types of materials created by the parent organization shall eventually be moved to archival storage. It helps control the flow of paper within an institution throughout a record's life cycle — from its creation to its disposition. Inventories and record-retention schedules detail how long papers should be kept and when they should be moved to alternate storage or destroyed. Institutional records are more likely to be saved for primary

---

113. Jutta Reed-Scott, "Collection Management Strategies for Archivists," *The American Archivist* 47.1 (Spring 1986): 26.
114. National Union Catalog of Manuscript Collections (http://www.loc.gov/coll/nucmc/).

purposes that support legal, fiscal, and administrative roles. However, like the collection development policy, the records management plan can also help retain records important to cultural posterity.

The collection development policy should provide a detailed description of what the repository collects, even if the collecting focus seems obvious. You must define the collection scope by indicating the region from which you collect, by whom the collections are created, which specific topics they cover, and in what formats. Many managers of repositories believe that just having a vague idea of what their repository should be collecting is good enough to move ahead with acquisitions. They feel that their focus is obvious enough that a general idea of their collecting strategy is all that is required. However, committing specific strategies to paper ensures that the obvious is obvious to everyone. It also helps us realize what may not be so apparent and what needs to be more clearly defined.

As with mission statements, collection development policies can and should be periodically reviewed and revised — they must advance with the times. As a collection grows, the institution's collection development policy must take into account how collections are evolving, how our neighbors are developing, what new roles we may play in the community, how researchers perceive us in light of changes in their research needs and techniques, and how our collections reflect changes in society. It is important to remember that collections progress and not only reflect past history, but also can reveal current trends that will become the history of the future. Even institutions focusing on particular periods that do not include our own lifetimes need to evaluate their collections and apply interpretations in terms of contemporary sensibilities. For our core collection to remain viable and worthwhile, we must consider what new materials and ideas we need to add to it as human knowledge expands and advances.

## Elements of a Collection Development Policy

The following is a list of elements that may be found in a collection development policy. Not all institutions include all of the items outlined here. Some may be placed in alternate administrative tools.

**Statement of Purpose** — As a training tool and for point of explanation, the purpose statement identifies the role the policy plays in the functioning of the institution. It establishes the need for such a policy to assist focus, acquisition, and deaccession. It cites the requirement to identify gaps and to set up collection collaboration with similar repositories. It confirms the value of collections, establishes the need to plan for them, and identifies the need for collection-building decision-making.

**Authorship Statement** — The authorship statement identifies who wrote the policy, his/her role in the museum, and when the policy was written and approved by the board of trustees or another appropriate governing body.

**Review Procedures** — These procedures describe the time frame for reviewing and revising the policy. They list who is responsible for ensuring that the policy is up to date and defines under what circumstances the policy will be changed or amended. They identify how the organization will know whether the policy is succeeding. Listed procedures assist actual practice by providing step-by-step directives to undertake when review is necessary.

**Mission Statement** — This statement succinctly describes the purpose of the repository. If the Archives is a department within a larger institution, an Archives' mission should explain the relationship of the department to the overall organizational mission.

**Scope of the Collections** — The scope describes in detail the focus of the collection. It explains why the institution collects what it does and defines its collecting niche. It identifies the breadth of the collecting effort with current and desirable levels of collecting activities. It also identifies the collection's current strengths and weaknesses. The scope describes types of materials that do not fit within the collection's span. It identifies important time periods for materials reflecting the development of its focus community, including dates of settlement, migration, industrialization, or single events (for example, disasters, construction projects, or discoveries). You can effectively list transitional actions in a timeline form.

**History of the Collections** — The history discusses how extant materials arrived in the collections and explains how decision-making processes about the collections were carried out up until this point. If necessary, the statement may explain why past methods of decision-making need to change.

**Collecting Goals and Objectives** — The goals and objectives outline acquisition priorities, including subjects, geographical regions, eras, and formats of materials. It aims to be specific and may even identify particular individuals or entities whose papers the institution seeks, if appropriate. It serves as a "wish list" for collecting and identifies collection gaps that are desirable to fill.

**Methods for Acquiring Collections** — The methods describe how a repository actively seeks donations, if it will purchase collections, and whether it accepts unsolicited donations, bequests, and collection exchanges with other repositories. The statement may include information about how resources will be obtained through fundraising or establishing relationships with donors. It lists activities needed to identify and locate desirable collections for accession.

**Donor Procedures** — The procedures list steps for reviewing collections offered by donors. They describe actions necessary for accepting collections from donors with reference to applicable laws concerning personal property and nonprofit organizations. The procedures outline how and when to refer inappropriate collections to alternate institutions. It describes legal, regulatory, or policy requirements of the institution that may affect potential donations.

**Accessioning Procedures** — The procedures list steps for formally accessioning and storing new collections in the Archives.

**Processing Procedures —** These procedures are often contained in a separate "Processing Manual" and describe steps for preparing archives for accessibility through preservation, arrangement, and description. They provide a time frame for processing — from the date of accession to a reasonable end date — to make records accessible.

**Users Statement** — This statement lists the types of people the repository aims to serve based on whom the Archives believes will be most interested in the collections it houses. It lists types of exhibits and programs that will be conducted by the Archives using parts of its collections and describes to whom these activities will appeal.

**Authority Statement** — This statement describes those responsible for acquiring and approving collections, including such people and bodies as the archivist, curator, director, board of trustees, and collections committee.

**Identification of Partner Institutions** — This section describes similar collections held by collecting partners to assist both those partners and the researchers trying to find them. It explains cooperative agreements that affect what collections are accepted and how the policy is implemented.

**Deaccessioning Procedures** — These procedures explain what materials can be deaccessioned and when. It describes if deaccessioned materials can be discarded, exchanged, donated, or sold and specifies that institutional personnel may not take possession of deaccessioned material. It describes if the collection can be used for alternate purposes within the institution, including uses that fall outside of standard collection development, such as hands-on education. It provides procedures for notifying donors if materials will be disposed and details how deaccessioning funds raised from selling off deaccessioned items should be used.

**Appraisal Guidelines** — These guidelines help repositories determine if particular collections are appropriate for accessioning into the repository's holdings. It also helps determine appropriate deaccessions when collections are under review.

---

## Appraising Collections

As noted earlier in this book, appraisal theory works as a tool to guide decisions about what materials we retain and what we discard. Some think, in a perfect world, we would keep all of the documents ever created. Yet, for reasons of space, access, and even legality, it is impractical and even undesirable to keep everything — there is a need to be discriminating. The collection development policy sets guidelines for considering which collections belong within your repository. Appraisal theory provides us with more details about how to consider particular materials. Whether the repository is large or small, is a dedicated Archives or a mixed repository, or is maintaining a geographic- or subject-focused collection, applying appraisal theory helps the institution make specific decisions about its collections. Using pertinent questions related to appraisal and the collection development policy as guides, an archivist can determine if a collection is an appropriate fit for the repository's scope. This section discusses how to ask the right questions and how to apply appraisal theory when an individual collection is under consideration. "[I]t sometimes seems that archivists and their colleagues hasten to acquire nearly any and all documentary remnants in the fear that they might be lost or some potential researcher deprived of their use, when, instead, they should develop a specific mechanism for determining when such records should be acquired and preserved."[115]

A cultural heritage professional must filter the repetitive, unimportant, and unrelated information out of

---

115. Cox, 40–41.

her holdings to create a useful documentary record. "Appraisal is THE critical archival act by archivists.... As archivists appraise records, they are determining what the future will know about its past; who will have a continuing voice and who will be silenced.... Archival appraisal decides which creators, functions, and activities generating records in society will be represented in archives, by defining, identifying, then selecting which documents and which media become archives in the first place."[116] Keeping everything makes it more difficult for users to find the information they seek, even with excellent cataloging and access tools. Keeping cultural heritage partners in mind, institutions must focus on the needs of their particular institutions, determining if the collection before them is a proper fit for their repository, if it would be more logical to refer the collection to another institution, or if it should be rejected outright.

In the archives field, the term "appraisal" refers to the evaluation of records for their historical worth to assess documents and determine those that should and should not be kept permanently. Differing from related fields, the term is not often used to connote a monetary assessment of a collection.[117] Appraisal of historical records focuses on the long-term informational and evidential value of materials and relates directly to the creation of an accurate documentary record. "Reducing quantity while condensing archival material qualitatively remains the task of the archivist as appraiser. It is the archivist alone who has the responsibility to create, out of this overabundance of

---

116. John Ridener, *From Polders to Postmodernism: A Concise History of Archival Theory* (Duluth, Minnesota: Litwin Books LLC, 2008). Quote included in foreword by Terry Cook.
117. Archivists are generally not involved in monetary appraisal and require an outside assessor to determine the monetary value of a collection for insurance purposes for the repository or for a donor tax benefit.

information, a socially relevant documentary record that is, in spatial terms, storable, and in human terms, usable."[118]

Like other collection development tools, the application of appraisal is subjective but must be steered by sound principles of archives management that can be made stronger by tying them directly to the institution's collection management policy. Whether a collection "fits" within the focus of the institution is the prime concern. Appraisal is a process that should involve understanding as much as you can about your collections, your collecting goals, and how a potential new donation or purchase fits within the broader picture. The goal for which we aim when we understand collection development and appraisal theory is to apply techniques that make our decisions less subjective, basing them more on developed methods and community understanding than cultural biases, to the extent that this is possible. "It goes without saying that the formation of a documentary heritage is a subjective and therefore socially conditioned process. Methods for limiting the effects of subjectivity must be employed, but these will never achieve a state of absolute objectivity — an impossible goal."[119]

To begin the process of appraisal, when evaluating whole collections, an archivist must view all prospective accessions as products of the activity for which they were created. Judge if the records provide significant information about people, places, or events defined in the repository's collection development policy. Remember, primarily, we are looking to develop our collections to fill gaps in the

---

118. Booms, 77.

119. Terry Cook, "Overview of Appraisal: Why Are We Here This Week," Presentation to Appraisal seminar. Monash University, Melbourne, VIC Canada. March 15, 1999 (http://www.recordkeeping.com.au/march99/terrycookoverview.html).

documentary record that we have vowed to keep in our community. What is important historically to one community may not be to another, and our collection development policy should serve as a guide describing what is important to us. Judge how integral the records are to a repository's mission and goals by posing questions that help determine their significance. Determine if incoming records add anything to a story we are already telling in our collections, and consider whether the records may help another repository tell their own stories.

To assess the value of a collection that fits within an institution's collecting guidelines, determine what is important to keep for its primary value, including administrative, legal, or fiscal purposes. These types of records are usually found in institutional, business, or government Archives. Then determine if there is any secondary value to the records, including their historical importance as evidence of a function of society or for the information they contain unrelated to the reasons for which the records were created.

In addition to the primary and secondary values of records, archives also may have intrinsic value. Intrinsic value refers to something with sentimental significance or some other intangible merit. Archives with intrinsic value have unique physical form, aesthetic or artistic appeal, exhibit use, substantial public interest because of a connection with a popular subject, or legal/administrative significance in its original form. In other words, consider whether the records have any worth just because of what they are, not because of the information they contain. A collection with strong informational value also should be evaluated for its intrinsic worth. In some cases, it may be appropriate to reformat and discard the original records if you do not have the space to house them and they have no intrinsic worth. In such a case, your organization may consider transferring the records to microfilm or digitizing them instead of accessioning the originals into your collections.

Age is not necessarily a prime indicator for materials' worth, but it can demonstrate intrinsic or informational value if few records from a particular time exist. Records do not always have to be old to have archival value; likewise, some old records have no value. They may have little informational content of significance if more extensive information appears elsewhere. The importance of old records lies in the fact that older documentation tends to be scarce because fewer records were created in earlier eras, and much of what did exist was destroyed over time. However, this is not always the case. Some old records are very common. Some of the documentation we consider routine today was also prolific in older eras and still exists in abundance today. A record collector should become familiar with some of the more common types of records to avoid collecting old materials that are easily found in other repositories, under the mistaken belief that they have intrinsic value because of their age.

An Archives must take into account whether a particular set of records and the information that it provides is useful to the researchers described in the organization's collection development policy. You must evaluate how a particular set of records relates to others in the collections, and whether records provide additional information about a topic that researchers expect to find in this repository.

The value of records is sometimes tied to their original arrangement and condition. For example, if there are two similar sets of records, an archivist may choose to keep the one that is better arranged and discard the second. Or, a set of records may be so badly arranged that it makes no sense and there is no value to the material. The cost of retention of ill-arranged or damaged materials often overrides our desire to keep something. It is important for an archivist to create a fiscal assessment of records considered for accession based on the work that will be involved in caring for them and the supplies and space involved in storing them. Determine the cost of collection care by estimating how long it will take to process the collection, what supplies are necessary to preserve materials, and how much space they will take up on shelves. Consider how much time it will take to process records based on how many other collections can be processed in the same amount of time. For example, if there is a large collection that will take the processing time of three other collections combined, determine if the informational value of the resources justifies taking time away from other work. If the collection is too expensive to maintain because of its size or because of preservation or conservation concerns, it should not be accessioned without realistic plans to raise money for its care and an intention to process it in a timely manner.

When Archives store potential donations for long periods of time before they actually accession them into their collections, they create a backlog of work and "quasi-accessioned" collections that fail the institution's responsibilities to their donors and patrons. Cultural institutions hold their accessions in trust to benefit society and are expected to safeguard cultural heritage.[120] Collections that have not been formally accessioned are not truly safeguarded. Their status remains in flux, and their documentation role has not been properly considered or defined. If an institution cannot afford to maintain a collection properly, if you do not have the time or money to

---

120. See John Rewald's passionate discussion of deaccessioning and the break of the "public trust" at the Metropolitan Museum of Art. "Should Hoving Be Deaccessioned," 1973, in Ed. Stephen E, Weil, *A Deaccession Reader* (Washington, D.C.: American Association of Museums, 1997): 23–37. The article focuses on art museums, but some of Rewald's concerns and his idea of "public trust" can be applied to records collected by our nation's Archives.

process and care for it, it is appropriate to help a donor seek out another institution that can.

An archivist should not add materials to her collection that are better suited to another institution's mission. It is important to have a collection development policy in place and to have started efforts of collaboration before appraising archives so that you have a thorough understanding of the scope of collecting practices. Taking into account the collections of partner institutions, the appraiser of an offered collection must consider if the collection, and those interested in it, would be better served if it were housed at a different institution.

To fill gaps identified in a collection development policy, it is to your greatest advantage to accept complete collections that provide as broad a view of a particular subject as possible. Split collections make it difficult to perform research and break the flow of information about a particular subject. The research value of a split collection is dramatically lower than that of an intact collection. Researchers must travel to view materials and may lose valuable clues about the thought process of the creator, just as they would with a collection in disarray. Keeping in mind that collections split among many institutions become diluted and less valuable for research, and that the most useful collections reflect their origin and the thought processes of their creators, full collections should be accessioned or passed on whole to other repositories. According to basic archival tenets and common sense, manuscripts are most valuable when they are stored intact and in the order in which the record creator kept them. If an Archives does not have the resources to provide for a whole collection intact, it should not accession any portion of the records.

A periodic review of an institution's collection development policy will allow it to see how well it is living up to its mission and collection development goals. It is a good idea to review new acquisitions annually and see how they fit in with the collection development policy. Analyze whether acquisitions fill identified gaps in collections or if they have brought a new dimension to a collecting focus that needs to be redefined in the policy. Look for new gaps in the holdings as materials are accessioned. Evaluate whether the repository's collection has become stronger in the past year, or if newly accepted materials have fallen outside of the scope of the collections policy.

## Appraisal Guidelines

These guidelines will assist with evaluating the appropriateness of accepting a specific set of records into a repository. To justify appraisal decisions, it is a good idea to keep written evidence of the thought process involved in accepting or rejecting a collection. This list of questions can help an appraiser ask pertinent questions about a collection, perform the research essential in determining the appropriateness of a collection, and prepare a written statement indicating why a particular decision was made. Use appraisal criteria as an outline, answering questions one by one, or use them as a guide to formulate a summary about appraisal decisions.

**Following Guidelines** — What do the records document? Do these records meet specific collection development guidelines outlined in the collection development policy? If so, which ones? If not, why are these records being considered? How do these records fit into your documentation strategy? Are there legal guidelines (i.e., retention schedules) for the management of these records?

**Filling Gaps** — Do these records fill a gap in the repository's collections? Do they duplicate other materials in the collections? Do they show an alternative view from an existing collection? Is the collection complete, or is it a portion of a complete collection? What is the relationship of these records to those in your current collection?

**Placing Value** — Are the records important to keep for administrative, legal, or fiscal purposes? Do they provide evidence of an event or activity in which the record creator was involved? What kinds of information do the records provide, and can this information be found elsewhere? Do the records have intrinsic value? Are these records being donated with any stipulations by the donor? Is the provenance of the material known? Are these vital records? In what format do these records exist? Does the information exist elsewhere in a more usable format? When and why were these records created? What is the significance of the records' content or the creator of the collection?

**Determining Rarity** — What time spans do the records cover, and does adequate documentation exist for this era? Is this a period specified for documentation in the collection development policy? Do the records tell us something about a group or individual for whom few records exist? What level of documentation already exists for this subject? Is more needed? Is the documentation uncommon?

**Seeking Researchers** — What use do you anticipate for these records? Which of the researchers described in your collection development policy would be most interested in this collection and why? How can you promote this collection for research use (e.g., exhibits or outreach opportunities)?

**Providing the Best Home** — Do these records match the collection goals outlined in your collection development policy, or would they be better matched to another repository's mission and collections policy? How do these records fit with your other collections or with those of another repository?

**Evaluating Available Resources for Processing** — Who will process this collection at your institution, and in what time frame? Can your institution afford the preservation and conservation requirements of this collection, or can you raise the money to afford it?

---

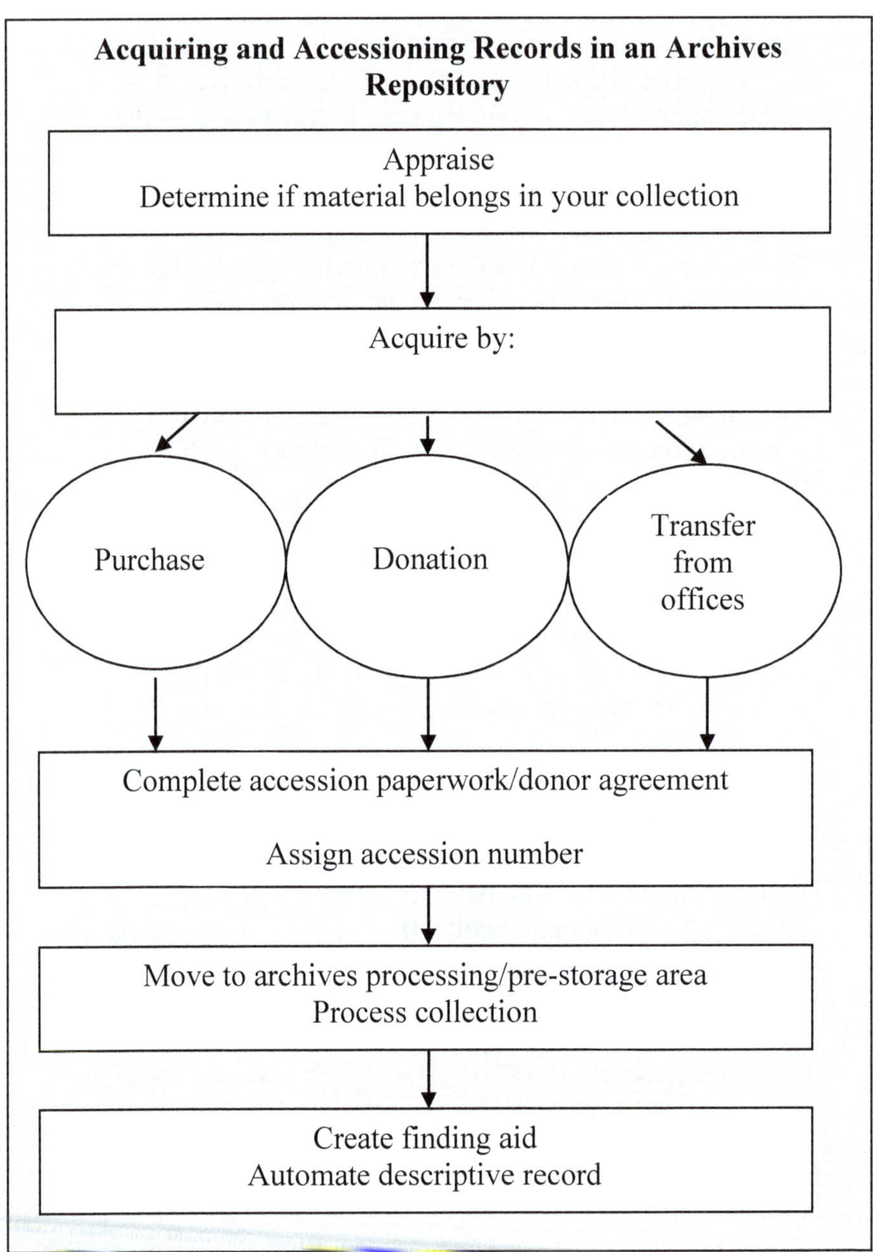

## Deaccessioning for Collection Development

Thoughtful deaccessioning procedures can be used to strengthen collections. When collections have been accessioned without the guidelines of a formal collection development policy, the materials often do not conform to an institution's mission or purpose. When it comes time to formalize a collecting strategy, we are sure to find previously accessioned archives that do not fit within our collecting scope. Deaccessioning allows us to apply appraisal techniques to these materials. This section discusses how to systematically reexamine your holdings by applying the methods of appraisal discussed earlier.

It is best to avoid controversy by carefully considering what you accession in the first place and thereby never or rarely having a need for deaccession procedures. However, it is likely that you will need to remove materials from holdings when reviewing collections to create a tighter focus. This is especially true for long-established repositories that operated over a period of time without a collection policy, accepting anything that was offered. From time to time, well-planned collections may even need to reconsider some of their possessions. Therefore, a description of deaccessioning procedures should be part of every collection development policy. All archives have collections that, by any reasonable appraisal standard, would not be accessioned today — collections that are redundant, fragmentary, or otherwise without redeeming informational content. Some were acquired through archival passivity, some through an indiscriminate collections program, and some for donor relations, but all were accepted in hopes that a more leisurely and thoughtful appraisal would be forthcoming. Unfortunately, to use Leonard Rapport's words, time has "burnished these records with a patina of permanence."[121] This makes repositories reluctant to withdraw them, but organizations would do well to reconsider their purpose within the repository.

During the process of creating or reviewing collection development policies, it is beneficial to identify those collections that do not fit within our defined scope — collections that were accessioned with little forethought, those that have not been formally accessioned, or those that do not fit into a newly defined focus. Deaccessioning should not be done on a regular basis but should be used as a tool only during rare times when a repository is (re)examining its collecting role and (re)writing collections policy. It is useful to consider removing incompatible collections from the repository's holdings to ensure that the institution's collection as a whole conforms to collecting guidelines. Strong deaccessioning rules need to be in place to ensure that deaccessioning is not done without considering the consequences. Removing inappropriate collections makes room for others that have more worth to the institution's mission and frees up staff time for better-suited materials.

The collection caretakers (the archivist, collections committee, etc.) may determine that a whole collection is appropriate for deaccessioning if it does not meet the repository's collection development guidelines, duplicates other materials in the collection, has deteriorated beyond repair, has conservation costs that would be prohibitive to the Archives budget, or is more appropriate for another repository's collection. Such decisions must not be based on the subjective whims of the sitting administration but

---

121. F. Gerald Ham, "Archival Choices: Managing the Historical Record in an Age of Abundance," *The American Archivist* 47. 1 (Winter 1984): 16. Rapport was a well-regarded archivist who spent most of his career at the National Archives. He specialized in eighteenth-century documents and wrote extensively on archival methods.

should relate to the established and defined role the institution plays in safekeeping the documentary record. Deaccessioning is one of the most serious issues with which an archival institution has to grapple, and it is among the most emotional. It can raise many questions among supporters outside of an institution. Researchers and patrons usually do not like to see materials removed from a collection. They often believe that important pieces of history will be lost.

It is up to the repository staff to educate the public about the purpose of deaccessioning. A clear collection development policy and effective public relations will help acquaint the public with the repository's long-range collecting goals and archival methods for accessioning and deaccessioning, making it easier to explain motivations regarding how we treat various collections. When dealing with donors, there is a need for us to thoroughly review potential donations in a timely manner and to make thoughtful decisions about whether or not these materials belong in our collections so we do not need to make more difficult deaccession decisions down the road. Collections accessioned into a repository with little thought are a hazard for the institution's good name and status in the collecting community, muddying our purpose and sense of community responsibility.

Collecting repositories must prepare donors to understand how Archives treat the materials that individuals desire to see permanently housed in our facilities. The institution's donor agreement form should contain a clause stating that the institution has the right to deaccession and dispose of materials as it sees fit. This clause should be enhanced by a more thorough description in the collection development policy of why the institution may need to turn down offered donations or deaccession holdings. Deaccessioning on a whim, deaccessioning that is perceived to happen for the wrong reasons, and haphazard appraisal can backfire and cause an Archives to lose potential future donations. Patrons do not want to think that their treasured bequests are at the mercy of a fickle institution. A donor who treasures his personal papers wants to think that the arrangements he makes for their safekeeping are permanent. We must assure those who give us their records that donations are as permanent as we can make them and that, if for some reason we do need to deaccession, we will take care to provide materials with another appropriate home.

"Before gifts can be sold, transferred, or discarded, the terms of the original gift must be reviewed carefully…a statement regarding deaccessioning and its moral and ethical implications must be part of every collection development policy."[122] If materials were brought into an institution informally and there is no donor form, a strong effort should be made to contact the donor to gain full, unencumbered rights to any undocumented collection we come across in our archives. Approval to deaccession donated items must be obtained from the donor or his or her heirs if such approval was not clearly noted in a donor agreement form. Such approval must be given in writing. If the donor agreement gives the repository the right to dispose of materials as it sees fit, the repository, as a courtesy, may choose to contact a living donor to inform him about the status of the collection. If the collection is not to be donated elsewhere or sold, and is instead scheduled for disposal, the donor may be given the option to reclaim his material.[123]

Deaccessioned materials should be withdrawn as collections, rather than withdrawing individual series or

---

122. Phillips, 36.

123. Archivists should encourage donors to talk to outside professionals for monetary appraisal information and must not provide such appraisals themselves. They should also encourage donors to talk to a qualified attorney about laws governing donations.

items within a collection. Breaking up original collections with one provenance destroys a collection's integrity. We lose thoughts inserted into the collection by the creator when we pick and choose which pieces of his work to keep. Separating series within a collection detracts from the informational value of the whole and can make the process of deaccessioning much more subjective. If a collection fits within collecting guidelines, then it should be accessioned in total and should not be deaccessioned in parts. You must not start removing pieces that seem less interesting or less applicable to the Archives' focus, or you endanger the informational value of the whole.

Archives may choose to sell, donate, trade, or discard collections that are found to be outside of their collecting scope, and each method has its own merits and problems. In the interest of preserving and enhancing the record, the preliminary choice may be to offer a collection to another cultural institution. Donating to or exchanging collections with partner institutions to strengthen our focus can also help strengthen ties among partnering institutions. Strong collaborative ties play an extremely important role in the area of deaccessioning, since collections tagged for removal are often valuable to another institution. One of the fears about deaccessioning is that a whole range of historical information can be lost. As with many other collecting decisions, deaccessioning should be done collaboratively with other institutions. This will assure that there is sufficient documentation in all areas of local history. "[D]eaccessioning questions can never be divorced from larger questions of collections management. Deaccessioning practices are inescapably intertwined with accessioning ones, and both must be framed within the larger structure of an institution's overall collections management policy."[124]

Collection caretakers may consider selling collections that duplicate those in other institutions and that are unwanted by your repository and sister institutions, but allowing items to leave the universe of publicly accessible cultural institutions can create controversy. Care must be taken to ensure that such materials are no longer needed to serve the public record and that their loss will not break the trust that the public has in cultural heritage institutions to safeguard their history.

By nature, archivists tend to see the value of their records in the information they provide and generally neglect or discount the monetary value of our holdings. In fact, as mentioned earlier, the word "appraisal" in the archival world rarely refers to finances and instead speaks to the idea of the value of records for history. However, when done appropriately, the sale of certain archival materials can raise monies to purchase supplies to care for valuable collections already in the Archives' custody. Generally, small archival institutions have funding problems, and we must not sell short the significant monetary value of materials that should not have been accessioned into our collections in the first place or do not fit with a reestablished collecting focus.

Bringing finances into the discussion of deaccessioning is distasteful to many and unethical to some. It should be a disposition method of last resort, with the sale of items ideally occurring only after collections have been offered to other repositories. We should not expect that all other nonprofits can pay as much as we may be able to get for collections sold in the private marketplace. We must determine, and make part of our

---

124. Ed. Stephen E. Weil, *A Deaccession Reader* (Washington, D.C.: American Association of Museums, 1997), 4.

deaccessioning policy, how we will deal with our collaborators — by donating, selling, or exchanging collections — and what we will do if the other repository is unable to accommodate our demands. When money is added to the mix, it is easy to lose sight that our first priority as an archival repository is to help record the history of our community and our country. "[B]y and large there are usually viable alternatives to commercial deaccessioning which give the future well-being of the deaccessioned object first priority."[125]

When it is indeed appropriate and ethical to sell our collections, we must also consider how the money raised from the sale of cultural materials that were once official accessions of an institution should be used properly. For example, some Archives have been known to sell off collections to raise capital that is used to implement the visions of management based on trends, without consideration of sound archival appraisal methods. At times, collections have been removed from institutions to support the whims of the current administration, such as raising money to install a trendy exhibition. Instead, clear guidelines must indicate how money raised from deaccessioning will help the Archives reach its long-term collecting goals. Money from the sale of archival materials should not be used to enhance nonarchival areas of collection development or other activities not related to archives. Ethically, funds garnered from selling deaccessioned collections should be used only for the preservation/conservation of existing archival materials. Materials fitting within the collection development guidelines must never be deaccessioned and sold to raise money to purchase other collections, even if the potential collection seems more desirable. The collections must not

---

125. Stephen H. Miller, "Selling Items from Museum Collections," ed. Stephen E. Weil, in *A Deaccession Reader*, 59.

be viewed as a cash cow for purchases and upgrades. Appropriate funds should be raised through fundraising and outreach activities.

As a matter of policy, in order to avoid a conflict of interest, items may not be sold to an employee of or an individual with any ties to an institution. Any materials for sale should be placed up for public auction after being offered to a collaborative repository, rather than offered directly to an individual or dealer. Such dealings always give a sense of impropriety. The public wants to see, and the cultural heritage institution should try to get, as much for a collection from a private individual as possible.

One of the most controversial areas of deaccessioning involves the permanent destruction of devalued materials. It is vital that all areas of appraisal decision-making have been carefully considered to ensure that a gap in the documentary record is not created with the destruction of material that is unwanted by a repository, its collaborators, and collectors. Care must be taken that items to be destroyed have no primary, secondary, or intrinsic value; are not in such poor shape that they no longer have value; and don't duplicate information found elsewhere in the documentary record. Original records destroyed in favor of keeping preservation copies must have no intrinsic value. Appraisal decisions related to deaccessioning items should be justified the same way that such decisions are made for new, incoming collections. It is a rare collection that has no value to anyone. Collections with no value for collecting purposes may be useful for education in schools, to Archives visitors, or to traveling exhibits. What seems worthless in archival terms may indeed have monetary value through a dealer familiar with collectors. Archival repositories would be wise to consider all the possibilities for their unwanted collections before turning to their destruction.

You must be prepared to give a good reason for all deaccessioning decisions by keeping meticulous records about items removed from the collections. Once a deaccession is documented with a thorough explanation of why it is being removed from the repository, the archivist must then defend the means of deaccession for administrative purposes and for possible public-relations reasons. There is always the possibility that those in charge of shaping a collection will be challenged for their decisions. The institution should establish formal written procedures for deaccessioning — to avoid any confusion among staff, management, and donors — about how deaccessioned materials will be handled. Information about deaccessions should be recorded and kept with other Archives administrative tools.

## Code of Ethics — Collection Management

Both the Society of American Archivists (SAA) and the Association of College and Research Libraries (ACRL) have little to say on the subject of deaccessioning and selling collections. The American Association for State and Local History's Code of Ethics and the American Association of Museums' ethics statements can serve as good guides for making collection decisions.[126]

The American Association for State and Local History (AASLH) Code of Ethics begins[127]:

Historical collections, including structures, are the bedrock upon which the practice of history rests. Association members shall always act to preserve the physical and intellectual integrity of their collections.

A. Institutions shall maintain and abide by comprehensive collections policies officially adopted by their governing authorities.
B. Priority shall be given to the care and management of collections.

---

126. SAA Code of Ethics for Archivists (http://www.archivists.org/governance/handbook/app_ethics.asp).
AAM Code of Ethics for Museums (http://www.aam-us.org/museumresources/ethics/coe.cfm).
ACRL Code of Ethics for Special Collections Librarians (http://www.rbms.info/standards/code_of_ethics.shtml).
AASLH Statement of Professional Standards and Ethics (http://www.aaslh.org/documents/AASLHProfessionalStandardsandEthics.pdf).
127. AASLH continues the discussion about the appropriate treatment of collections in a variety of position papers. Most notably, *Ethics Position Paper 1 – The Capitalization of Collections* provides more information about element C. of the Code, which states collections shall not be capitalized or treated as financial assets.

C. Collections shall not be capitalized or treated as financial assets.
D. Collections shall not be deaccessioned or disposed of in order to provide financial support for institutional operations, facilities maintenance, or any reason other than the preservation of acquisition collections.
E. Collections shall be acquired, cared for, and interpreted with sensitivity to their cultural origins.
F. It is important to document the physical condition of collections, including past treatment of objects, and to take appropriate steps to mitigate potential hazards to people and property.

With regard to collections, the American Association of Museums Code of Ethics States[128]:

The distinctive character of museum ethics derives from the ownership, care, and use of objects, specimens, and living collections representing the world's natural and cultural common wealth. This stewardship of collections entails the highest public trust and carries with it the presumption of rightful ownership, permanence, care, documentation, accessibility, and responsible disposal.
Thus, the museum ensures that:

- Collections in its custody support its mission and public trust responsibilities
- Collections in its custody are lawfully held, protected, secure, unencumbered, cared for, and preserved

---

128. 

- Collections in its custody are accounted for and documented
- Access to the collections and related information is permitted and regulated
- Acquisition, disposal, and loan activities are conducted in a manner that respects the protection and preservation of natural and cultural resources and discourages illicit trade in such materials
- Acquisition, disposal, and loan activities conform to its mission and public trust responsibilities
- Disposal of collections through sale, trade, or research activities is solely for the advancement of the museum's mission; proceeds from the sale of nonliving collections are to be used consistent with the established standards of the museum's discipline, but in no event shall they be used for anything other than acquisition or direct care of collections
- The unique and special nature of human remains and funerary and sacred objects is recognized as the basis of all decisions concerning such collections
- Collections-related activities promote the public good rather than individual financial gain
- Competing claims of ownership that may be asserted in connection with objects in its custody should be handled openly, seriously, responsively, and with respect for the dignity of all parties involved

---

---

## Documenting a Deaccessioned Collection

List the reasons for deaccessioning material and record in detail the rules and procedures relating to the deaccession. Be prepared to explain how deaccessioning procedures strengthen the focus and research value of the overall collections. The archivist must be prepared for questions about motives and decisions.

- Describe the collection

- Cite the reason for its deaccession (e.g., collection does not fit within collection development guidelines, collection is better suited for another repository, collection is in poor condition)

- State what will happen to the material after it is deaccessioned (e.g., collection will be sold, transferred, traded to another repository)

- Record the reason why the collection will be handled in this manner and list other repositories contacted for possible interest in the collection

- If the material is in good condition and is to be discarded, describe collections that duplicate information found within or list procedures that will be taken to ensure information is not lost (e.g., via microfilm or digitizing)

- Cite the date and the authority for the deaccession (i.e., who approved it)

- Record the date when the donor was contacted and attach a copy of the letter sent to the donor notifying him about the deaccession

- List any applicable rules or regulations regarding the deaccessioning of this collection (e.g., according to donor agreement, the repository has clear title to the collection; the collection meets the definition of "abandoned cultural property" within one's state, giving the repository the right to dispose of the material as it sees fit)

---

## The Archival Survey and Assessment

This section discusses the need for a comprehensive examination of collections and outlines the elements one must include in such a study. Information about surveying is placed as the last section in this book so that readers may jump from here to begin their archival programs. The survey ties together all other concepts previously introduced, and its implementation should be made easier by the strategies found in this book. The surveyor will benefit from an overall understanding of collection theory and an awareness of the context in which we make decisions. As the archivist identifies materials in an existing collection, she can think about the role the archives play in the overall documentation of community and collection development.

The preliminary challenge for any community embarking on a collaborative collection development project is recognizing a shared imperative for promoting culture among diverse repositories. It is also challenging to convince those with a related interest in preserving our cultural heritage to work in partnership with others. An archival survey provides a society with information about its collective cultural resources, enabling it to examine the history retained in its repositories. It should be used to guide the development or restructuring of collecting policies and can help convince towns of the need for collaborative programs. A repository will generally perform survey work as an introductory step toward gaining control over its collections.

The archival survey defines where your organization stands, where it needs to go, and how it can get there. It is a starting point for an institution, regardless of the state of its collections. Archives are in danger due to neglect, mishandling, and other factors. The survey allows you to take an objective look at how to save the materials in a repository's possession, propelling a community to more thoughtfully consider and better care for the cultural resources. Many institutions hesitate to tackle collection problems out of ignorance or embarrassment. There is always more for any institution or collection caretaker to learn; there is always a repository in worse shape. You must start caring for materials, whatever the state of your collections. If an institution begins thinking about collections and making plans to care for them today, they can turn around any situation. Do not neglect materials in the future just because they were neglected in the past.

A preliminary record survey (or assessment) within a single repository allows you to get a better idea of the extent of your collections and the problems associated with them. "Collecting, in the strictest definition of the term, is not the first order of business in preserving local historical resources. The basis, the foundation, the sine qua non, the bottom line of any preservation program, is the identification of culturally significant resources. Obviously, before a historical resource can be collected or singled out for preservation, it must first be identified. And, ideally, the decision on what to collect and preserve should not be made until all cultural resources in a particular locale are identified. It is impossible for any local group to preserve every historical resource — every building, every site, every document, every photograph, and every artifact — in a given locale."[129] Organizations must work together to gain a complete understanding of their community to guarantee satisfactory documentation of their locale.

---

129. Robert J. Bailey, "Grassroots History: Collecting and Preserving," *Journal of Mississippi History* 40 (1978): 204–205, quoted in Robert J. Cox's *Documenting Localities: A Practical Model for American Archivists and Manuscript Curators* (Lanham, Maryland: Scarecrow Press, Inc., 1996): 44–45.

A survey allows an Archives to get a better look at its place in the archival community by helping the institution compare its collections to those around them. Survey work involves examining collections, determining the scope of records, the amount of space that they comprise, costs involved with storing materials, any preservation issues that archival resources have, and their general arrangement. The survey will also help those managing the archives to identify the collection's current focus and ascertain strengths and weaknesses, such as ill-documented themes and dates of missing records in a long series. "Archivists must know something of this larger body of documentation if they are to select their archives with competence, to assist researchers to the fullest extent, and to plan sound archival programs. The records survey is a primary means by which archivists gain this knowledge."[130]

According to well-respected archivist John A. Fleckner, the records survey serves six purposes. The first is to foster administrative efficiency, which calls attention to the need for the better care of an organization's records and can set a well-rounded archives program in motion. Second, the survey aids researchers by promoting access to materials. Third, it promotes preservation of archival material. Fourth, it furthers collection development of local collections through its findings. Pertinent to the processes described in this book, the survey provides information that can be used to improve the planned collecting a collections policy facilitates. Additionally, survey work helps strengthen cross-professional and community ties, develops inter-repository cooperation, and strengthens understanding of the need for collaborative collecting programs. Finally, the survey helps educate students and others about primary

---

130. John A. Fleckner, *Archives and Manuscript Surveys* (Chicago: Society of American Archivists, 1977), 1.

sources and archival methods, laying a foundation for diverse individuals and institutions to properly care for archival resources.[131]

**Records Survey Purpose According to John A. Fleckner**

1. To Foster Administrative Efficiency
2. To Aid Researchers
3. To Promote Preservation of Archival Materials
4. To Further a Collecting Program
5. To Improve Planning for Archival Programs
6. To Educate and Train

For collaborative purposes, the survey allows record collectors to get a better sense of what documentation exists in a community, encouraging a broad perspective of available resources related to the history of a region or subject. The survey therefore serves as a bridge toward creating a full community documentation plan. An extensive, collaborative survey of organizations throughout a community allows you to verify what is available in local repositories, how collections overlap, and how your repository's resources fit among many. When performed in association with a documentation project, a survey can help you analyze existing records and influence record-making practices.

Any weaknesses identified will guide a collaborative group to defining what information needs to be collected that is not currently being targeted and what information needs to be created to complete the

---

[131] Fleckner's examination of records surveys for the SAA Basic Manual series is the most fundamental authority on this subject (3–6).

documentary record that is currently not being recorded. One of the goals of a survey is to uncover all the positive aspects of a collection and its negatives. You should not aim to hide the flaws but to fix them. An archival assessment should be honest, so that the information can be used in the future to benefit individual organizations and the collaborative. Some find it necessary to use an impartial outsider, such as a consultant, to perform the role of surveyor so that they can truly be forthcoming and thorough. A written summary of a collection based on survey findings that identify strengths and weaknesses is helpful when writing institutional policies and when working with others to better define a repository's role in the community.

Survey work involves examining repository records directly and listing information about what you find. This includes details about the records themselves, such as their subjects, creation dates, creators, where material is located, arrangement, and current preservation status of materials. The survey should also provide details about the repository itself, such as space available and the storage environment. A comprehensive study will also examine the overall management of the repository and discuss the archives' role within the institution, the records' relationship to other collections, available staffing, and evaluation of management tools. Once all of this information is gathered, the surveyor(s) should consider the future of materials and make recommendations about collection growth, care, accessibility, and appraisal.

During an assessment, it is necessary to have an understanding of archival theories of arrangement and access so a collection may be evaluated based on professional standards. Primarily, the assessment should aim to keep donations created by an individual or institution together to maintain provenance. While identifying records during the survey, you must primarily note materials on the fonds and series levels but also must aim to gain an awareness of how the whole collection fits together. Begin to evaluate the effectiveness of the arrangement of the collection as a whole. Examine if the arrangement of record groups and series highlights the collections or causes confusion about record provenance and relationships. Note if similar materials are stored together or if they are spread out all over storage areas without any cohesion. While assessing a collection, you must consider how to physically and intellectually arrange collections to highlight connections while maintaining the provenance of materials.

The most difficult part of a records survey or assessment is recognizing the need to keep a unique collection with a distinct provenance intact while balancing this with the need to define similarities among materials. An assessment allows you to gain an overall understanding of the repository's holdings in total, while defining connections on paper. The description of a repository's holdings should include information about the current arrangement of collections with suggestions for alternate arrangements through intellectual and physical control. Experiment in writing with various different ways to think about (i.e., mentally organize) the collections to find the way that seems to best highlight the collections' focus. The survey should identify the record groups and series within a repository, as well as subseries and items that are particularly important.

**Levels of Arrangement for Surveying Records**

**Repository** – Describes the organization caring for the materials: the "Archives."

**Record group (fonds)** – A body of related records established based on provenance. The record group generally refers to the institutional body, such as an agency or department that created the records, or to an individual creator. The record group is sometimes also called a collection. Together, the numerous collections contained within a repository are called the repository's collection.

**Series** – A group of files or documents maintained together as a unit because they are related to a particular subject or function, result from the same activity, or have a common form. Series usually are identified by a common filing order, subject matter, or physical type (e.g., correspondence, minutes, receipts, and drawings). The series level is particularly important because it expresses the character of the collection. Additionally, the final description of a collection focuses largely on the series level, and thus is of particular interest to researchers.

**File unit** – Refers to how items are placed for filing purposes. Units may be file folders, bound volumes, disks, tubes, reels, etc. File folders, the most common unit at this level, usually are arranged in alphabetical, chronological, geographical, subject, or numerical order.

**Item** – Refers to individual documents such as letters, memos, and reports found within file units.

A written summary of the collections should be based on information gathered with an overview of the collections. The summary should aim to describe the role of each collection within its parent organization and community. The author should make recommendations for appraisal, including points to be considered for a collection development policy, gaps and strengths in the collections, and recommendations for deaccession (if appropriate). She should further make recommendations to facilitate access, including written finding aids and proprietary databases. The summary must list preservation concerns to be addressed, including environmental considerations and specific problems with individual series or record groups. The report shall also include an evaluation of current management tools and a description of other appropriate tools, including accession registers, policy and procedure manuals, finding aids, and automated databases. It must further evaluate the organization's institutional archives and recommendations for records management to preserve the organization's history. A comprehensive document will also include digital photographs of the collections to be used as "before" pictures showing the state of the collections prior to action upon the consultant's recommendations. These can later be used to demonstrate need and to show improvements once they are made. A final survey report may also include a strategic plan with future goals and suggestions for training needed so staff can properly care for collections.

For community documentation purposes, the survey has vital elements that can help institutions gain a strong understanding of each repository in a community. In addition to reviewing known holdings within a repository or institution, an archivist or collaborative may seek to identify collections outside of their realm. Surveys can involve reaching out to private citizens to identify records in private hands. Surveyors can perform interviews using a form to identify important community holdings. "The form increases the consistency and accuracy of survey returns by stating the specific items of information the surveyor is seeking and making gaps in responses obvious. The form also facilitates editing and arranging survey findings."[132]

Though it can be beneficial to hire a consultant to assist with this initial work, organizations without immediate resources to hire outside help can begin the survey process on their own using the guidelines outlined here. The survey will set the foundation for success in all areas of archives management and collaborative collection development.

---

132. Fleckner, 13.

## Survey Form

You perform a survey by browsing through all the archival materials in your possession. Gather as much information as possible in a brief form. Record the location of records, noting common themes and record creators. Records should be identified as part of larger and smaller groupings of material within an institution. The surveyor must consider that five different levels of these groupings exist according to professional archives standards — moving from larger to smaller — and that these levels form the basis of arrangement for all collections. These levels include repository, record group, series, file unit, and item.

- Record the date of the survey.
- Record the name of the person performing the survey.
- Write the location of the records (preferably a bay and/or shelf number, but if collections are not organized, write "closet in hall," "file drawer in secretary's drawer" — whatever is appropriate).
- Describe the type of storage equipment used — e.g., vertical files, lateral files, archives boxes, record boxes.
- If materials are maintained in boxes, number each box and record the number of boxes.
- Check all of the types of materials found in the collection/records groups.
- Record the total cubic feet of the collection/records group being reviewed.
- Describe how the collection is arranged. Is it alphabetical? Chronological? Is it arranged by subject? Does it have varying arrangements?
- Record the name of the contact person(s). This person cares for the records, created the records, or is in charge of them.

- Record the department or organization that created the records if an institutional collection is under review. If it is a collection of personal papers, record the name of the person who created the collection.
- Summarize the series found in the collection. In other words, record how the collection is broken down into subject or another alternate arrangement.
- Describe the series in detail by listing important groups of records, highlights of the collection, inclusive dates, and other noteworthy aspects of the collection.
- Briefly describe the condition of the collection. Note any obvious preservation issues and how to address them.
- Note any obvious missing documentation (i.e., missing run of dated material, overlooked subjects, etc.).
- Try to take photographs showing the current condition of the collection. This is very useful for a "before" look at the collections if extensive work is planned to improve the housing or storage of materials.
- If the surveyor is aware of similar collections outside of the institution, list related series. Describe the related collection and its relationship to this one.
- Comment about the current condition of the collections and briefly discuss how to improve it. Note any other concerns or observations.

---

## Questions for Identifying Local History Resources

For community documentation purposes, archivists must develop appropriate questions for surveying records outside of their custody that are held by associations, small businesses, and individuals. Responses should be attained through informational interviews with record creators or by examining the records themselves. These questions may also help repositories examine their own holdings:

- Name of the interviewer and the date
- Name of the interviewee(s) and name of the organization(s) they represent (if applicable)
- Describe the types of records you create in each category
- Business/financial (account books, invoices, etc.)
- Correspondence/memos (incoming and copies of outgoing correspondence, e-mail)
- Publicity (brochures, press releases, news articles)
- Documentary (photographs, diaries, scrapbooks, videos, oral histories)
- Other
- Which of these records do you keep indefinitely?
- What types of records do you keep that you did not create? Describe types, formats, and how they came into your possession
- What are the dates of the records in your care?
- By whom were each series of records created?
- How do you make decisions about which records to keep? How do you organize the ones that you keep? (i.e., describe your filing system)
- In what formats would one find your records?
- How do you preserve your records? (i.e., what housing materials do you use and where do you keep them?)

- Have you ever inventoried your records? Do you keep an index of your collection?
- Have you identified any records in your collection that you think have particular historical importance? Please identify and explain why you think they are important
- Do you take special precautions to care for records that you think have historical importance?
- What records would you like to collect that you are not currently collecting?
- Do you know of any gaps in your holdings?
- Do you know of anyone collecting similar records?
- Size of the collection
- Additional comments

---

## Model 8

## A Business Valuing Its History:

### Hershey Community Archives

The Hershey Chocolate Company, now The Hershey Company, was established in 1894 in Lancaster, Pennsylvania. More than seventy-five years after its founding, and almost fifty years after Milton Hershey started his popular Hershey Museum, the famed corporation supported the development of the Hershey Community Archives. The Hershey entities today include: the Hershey Company, Hershey Entertainment and Resorts Company, Hershey Trust Company, Milton Hershey School, and the M.S. Hershey Foundation. In 1981, these five entities and the Hershey Museum (now named The Hershey Story and operating as a division of the M.S. Hershey Foundation) came together with a purpose of identifying and preserving records of Milton Hershey's work.

The Hershey entities always valued their history, and Milton Hershey had been a strong proponent of promoting cultural heritage and lifelong education. Hershey worked to build institutions and a local infrastructure that could better the lives of his workers. The Hershey Company home page even states this ideal: "For more than 100 years, the Hershey Company has been a leader in making a positive difference in the communities where we live, work and do business."[133] The idea for an Archives in the late twentieth century could easily be supported amid

---

133. The Hershey Company Web site (http://www.thehersheycompany.com).

such strong traditions and a strong appreciation for community roots.

Located in what is now the town of Hershey, the Hershey Community Archives is an operating division of the M.S. Hershey Foundation and formed as a nonprofit to benefit the community and the Hershey entities. Initial work on the archives involved surveying, collecting, and processing the historical records of several Hershey entities so that they could be made available to researchers. Space was secured for work, and a building was designed for the records' permanent housing. Initial planning recognized a strong connection between the work of the Hershey Museum and the Archives. A joint repository was envisioned for the two, but this was not to become reality until 2009, when the museum was renamed The Hershey Story and these separate Hershey nonprofits were brought under one roof on Chocolate Avenue so that they could more easily share ideas and accommodate researchers. Despite their physical proximity, the Hershey Community Archives and The Hershey Story are independent bodies with separate collections. Members of Hershey business entities serve on an advisory board for the Archives and contribute to the repository's budget, while The Hershey Story has a separate board.

The original Hershey Museum contained North American Indian and Pennsylvania German artifact collections that Milton Hershey purchased. In the 1980s, it expanded its work to incorporate Hershey-related materials. Based on the results of numerous visitor surveys, peer reviews, and focus groups, the board of managers of the M.S. Hershey Foundation approved a change of mission to focus on Milton Hershey, his business, community, and philanthropies in 2007. The records within the Archives help the museum with its interpretive mission. Both repositories work cooperatively with the Pennsylvania Historical and Museum Commission and the Hershey-

Derry Township Historical Society (which was established in 1991 soon after the Hershey Community Archives, with broader goals that sometimes overlap), as well as with other historic sites.

In addition to its work with the historical records of Hershey entities, the Hershey Community Archives collects the records of local associations such as the Hershey Rotary Club and the Hershey Figure Skating Club. This arrangement is mutually beneficial, helping Hershey live up to its goal of making a positive difference in its community and strengthening its research collections, while helping groups with ever-changing boards to centralize their materials and keep them safe. The Archives is also actively conducting an oral history program. With more than 400 recordings among their holdings, they are building a collection of first-person accounts that fill gaps in the Hershey story.

The Hershey entities recognize the value of preserving history through the proper maintenance of historical records and archives. Cultural heritage resources are seen as a valuable asset for Hershey to tell its own story and reach out to the public. Materials since the Archives' inception are used for promotion and marketing, to protect corporate trademark assets, to celebrate milestones, and to enhance exhibits.

Though it took the Hershey entities many decades to embark on an archives management program, and even more to realize a centralized facility for maintaining cultural heritage resources, the business of Hershey was eventually able to support community documentation efforts that can serve as a model for other businesses and communities.

## Model 9

## Valuing History to Promote Preservation:

### St. Johnsbury, Vermont

"The St. Johnsbury Archives Collaborative is a partnership between five institutions: the St. Johnsbury Academy, the St. Johnsbury Athenaeum, the Fairbanks Museum and Planetarium, the Town of St. Johnsbury, and the St. Johnsbury Historical Society. The collaborative was formed in 1999 to exchange information about the partners' holdings of historic records and to develop a strategy for preserving St. Johnsbury's heritage."[134] The St. Johnsbury Archives Collaborative is an example of a town achieving a lot when a small window of opportunity arises and the stage is set for cooperation.

Recognizing the importance of their history, the collaborative planned extensively for, pursued, and received a three-year grant from the National Historical Publications and Records Commission through its local State Historical Record Advisory Board (SHRAB). The grant enabled the partnering institutions to hire a roving project archivist who surveyed records at the various repositories in town, trained project participants in processing, and provided guidelines for the care and use of materials in St. Johnsbury. The consultant defined differences among the collections of the various institutions, helping them to better understand the scope of what they are collecting and how each institution

---

134. For more on the St. Johnsbury Archives Collaborative, see Gregory Sanford and Ann Lawless, "Regrants and Collaboration: A View from Vermont's North Kingdom," *Annotation* (NHPRC newsletter, Vol. 29, No. 1, March 2001).

contributes to the maintenance of St. Johnsbury's rich history.

Serving a community of 7,500, the collaborative upholds the forward-thinking motivations of the Fairbanks family, which brought its business and philanthropy to town in the nineteenth century. Thaddeus Fairbanks endowed some of the institutions where the most important archival records related to town history now reside. (For example, the museum itself began as a place for Fairbanks to display his personal collections.) Throughout town, the family left a strong appreciation for culture and cooperation to boost cultural endeavors and education. Though today funding for the care of historical records is minimal, the strong sense of community and history exuded by the institutions in town help ensure the longevity of an archives program.

The collaborative has created a "Guide to Historic Records" for the repositories, summarizing by subject the scope of documentation for St. Johnsbury and the collection strengths. More detailed information about holdings and cataloging records have been added to a statewide database. In addition to the collaborative collections, the document cites where more historical documentation can be found, including the local court, churches, cemeteries, businesses, clubs, and private individuals. The collaborative has also recently worked to educate the public about the use of St. Johnsbury's records through a series of lectures and workshops.

The strong work of the original consulting archivist helped boost staff members' appreciation for the archives in their care, helping them recognize how the archives support other collections and can be a boon to community outreach. Collaborative participants say that "the word is out" and realize that their project made it more "trendy" to promote history. Restaurants began to use the archives to find photos to decorate their walls, more people began using materials for research, and researchers contributed to collections with the results of their work.

Despite limited sources for continuing large-scale archives projects, the groundwork has been set. Records are stored in the best environments possible for now — in archival boxes and rooms where climate remains relatively stable. They are safe from harm and are accessible. St. Johnsbury has formed a good foundation of collections that reflect its cultural identity. It also has solid ideas about the future of its historic records when money again becomes available. The legacy of valuing archives is firmly in place due to the collaborative's forethought and efforts. Its example shows how federally funded and local programs, along with philanthropic individuals, can do much to promote the value of archives, providing windows of opportunity that towns such as St. Johnsbury can turn into successful documentation endeavors.

# Conclusion

Cultural heritage repositories have an awesome responsibility to ensure that the history of our civilization is preserved for future generations. Their archival records hold a key for deciphering our culture. Anxious to gather copious materials for education, research, and outreach, many organizations create unfocused collections that hinder their abilities to present a balanced view of society. Instead, they should work to present a focused visage to their audience by gaining control of a core asset, aiming to build collections that purposefully fill a well-defined niche.

Documentation of our culture is important to better understand ourselves and our society. Archives that provide diversified primary information about communities help individuals evaluate the past for themselves so they can better understand current events. Documents ensure a smoothly running society by a government and citizenry we can hold accountable to our laws. Cultural heritage fosters a sense of community and civic pride. It ties us to the past and helps develop our sense of purpose for the future. For these reasons and myriad others cited in this book, it is an archival repository's duty to ensure that thorough documentation of communities is identified, evaluated, preserved, and made accessible to people in a democratic society.

Within any given community, people are constantly creating, maintaining, and using records. From the individuals, businesses, and organizations that create written documentation in the course of their daily routines to the professional repositories that collect material culture, there is a need for proactive identification of records that are most important to the understanding of ourselves and our activities. Working together as cultural heritage partners, an informed citizenry can help the archivist establish and preserve meaningful collections that tell about our past and describe the time and place in which we live to benefit ourselves and our descendants.

We must show deference to the integrity of our collections and work to create a complete documentary story of our civilization across media. To accomplish this task, we must value both older formats and newer technologies for creating and providing access to material cultural. Cultural heritage partners need to attach value by appraising collections in whatever formats we find them. Partners must step beyond their individual institutions and focuses of study to see a bigger picture and understand how their specialization fits within a larger historic and modern cultural heritage and information society. Professionals must share expertise with colleagues from related fields who deal with diverse resources, respecting differences and finding new ways to bring together sometimes dissimilar practices. Cultural heritage collaborators must value the records in their possession for their independent potential as information sources or as supporting resources for other diverse collections.

Partners can accomplish the task of documenting society by implementing proper, well-tested procedures for creating and administering holdings. An institution can form deliberate, logical, and worthwhile archival collections that easily draw attention to the organization's role by basing collection development on a policy that grows from a well-formed mission statement. In forming their collections, cultural heritage institutions will benefit from partnering with repositories that maintain similar materials and from the use of archival principles that have been developed over the past century. Repositories will profit from the use of tools identified in this book such as community-wide archival surveys that help them understand the strengths and weaknesses of their holdings, aid with locating materials, and prepare individuals to identify aspects of society that have not been properly documented.

Additional tools grounded in developing theory can help partners come closer to meeting an ultimate goal of full documentation for their chosen concentration. The adapted community documentation strategy described in this book will help collaborators work together to ensure that attempts are made to gather, preserve, and make accessible all items with enduring value, facilitating the study of a complete documentary record to the extent it is possible. In a society that is swiftly changing as documentation becomes more abundant and ephemeral, professionals need to work more closely with record creators to see how tried-and-true practices of archives management can use grounded theory to ensure the longevity of our cultural heritage. Working together, we can rely on individuals' expertise, varied views, and creativity born of specialized knowledge to adapt strategies that accommodate changing needs due to diverse collections and new expectations for communication and collaboration.

This book encourages cultural heritage repositories to aim for success by creating strong collections that are reflective of a community and by providing ready access to these materials. To achieve success, institutions must ensure that they have monetary resources and personnel necessary to accomplish everyday tasks and long-range visions. They must invoke citizen recognition of the repository as a vital entity that reflects the community's sense of identity. Such success is not achieved overnight, but must be worked toward through thoughtful planning, outreach, and partnerships.

*Cultural Heritage Collaborators: A Manual for Community Documentation* has provided an overview of the role of archival material for preserving our cultural heritage. It outlines the tools necessary to systematically collect with collaborative partners those documents that possess permanent value. The stories of the Wenham Museum, Danvers Archives, Winchester Historical Society and Archives, Gloucester Archives, Churchill County Museum, Montana Traveling Archivists program, Marist College Environmental Archives, Hershey Community Archives, and St. Johnsbury Archives Collaborative presented in these pages are models, but they are not unattainable. Their examples illustrate that anyone can work to build their archival programs, sometimes with outside assistance, but that a successful program does not build itself. If you take anything from this book, please understand these things: First, it does not matter how your community maintains its archives now. Also, there is no one way to achieve "success." Finally, and most importantly, the achievements of your archives program will be built upon your community's individual culture and your own hard work from this day forward. The information in this book is designed to assist you with your successful future as a vital cultural heritage partner.

# Glossary of Selected Professional Archives Terminology

Accession — A group of records or archives from the same source, with the same provenance, accepted into an archive repository's holdings at the same time. The process of formally accepting the material is called accessioning. Materials are ascribed a unique, permanent accession number that aims to get material under basic archival control.

Acquisition — The materials added to a collection through transfer, donation, or purchase.

Appraisal — The process of determining the permanent value of records and thus where they end up at the end of their active lives. The determination of value is based on the evidence and information the records provide, their arrangement and condition, intrinsic worth, and relationship to other records.

Active Records — Records that are regularly used in the course of an institution's or individual's regular activities. Such records can be used daily, weekly, or monthly and should be maintained in offices where they can be readily accessed and not within archival repositories. Some active records may be deemed important for posterity (as archives) and should be moved to an Archives once they are no longer regularly needed.

Archival Survey — A formal project conducted to determine the scope of materials in an institution or community.

Archives —
1. Materials relating to the history of an institution that are kept for permanent preservation because of their evidential or informational value (e.g., documents, photographs, books, maps, blueprints).
2. The location at which archival materials are maintained.
3. The organization that cares for archival materials (i.e., the people, archivist, manuscript curator).

Arrangement — The organization of archival material following a five-level standard hierarchy that includes repository, fonds, series, subseries, and items.

Artifact — Nonarchival materials (objects) retained because of their historical value. They are generally maintained by a curator rather than an archivist.

Artificial Arrangement — An organizational scheme applied to a record collection by an archivist and not by the collection's original creator.

Collection — The contents of an Archives or a specific large group of materials within that Archives.

Collection Development Policy — The document that defines what an institution collects and what it does not. It sets a direction for the collecting focus of the organization by expanding on the mission statement.

Cultural Heritage — Tangible items that are considered worthy of preservation for the future due to their reflection of a society's identity. It also encompasses intangible values and customs that are passed from one generation to another.

Cultural Heritage Institution — An institution that stores materials that represent a society's intellectual and artistic essence and supports the continuance of that society's traditions and memory.

Cultural Heritage Partner — A person interested in sustaining cultural heritage or one who possesses tangible or intangible cultural heritage items and/or rituals.

Deaccession — The process of formally removing items from a collection.

Descriptive Inventory — A basic tool created by archivists to describe and facilitate access to a collection. A descriptive inventory (i.e., collection guide or manuscript inventory) defines the scope of a collection and its details.

Documentary Record — The surviving written or otherwise recorded information that provides evidence or information about a society and its activities in a certain time and place.

Donor Agreement Forms — Documents used to legally transfer material to a collecting repository and to reach out to potential record creators to explain the importance of preserving archives in their care.

Ephemera — Items that are created for a specific event or activity, are often mass-produced, and are not intended to survive indefinitely (e.g., a handbill, newspaper, or menu).

Evidential Value — In archival "appraisal," the worth of a record based on its reflection of the organization and the function of the institution or body that created it. Records possessing evidential value provide authentic and adequate evidence of an organization's activities.

Finding Aids — Indices to a collection that help establish intellectual control over the archives. Basic finding aids include descriptive inventories, guides, accession registers, card catalogues, shelf lists, and automated databases.

Historical Value — The worth of material based on its importance to the cultural heritage.

Informational Value — In archival appraisal, the worth of a record based on the information it contains.

Institutional Archives — The records collected to document the history of an institution such as a government body, business, or nonprofit organization.

Intellectual Control — The management of archives through descriptive documents resulting from the process of arrangement and description.

Intrinsic Value — The worth of material based on monetary or sentimental value.

Material Culture — Any physical item created by a person or a society that possesses "historical value."

Mission Statement — A declaration that defines the purpose of an institution or program.

Natural Collection — A collection of materials arranged on the principles of "Provenance" and "Sanctity of Original Order."

Personal Papers — Materials relating to an individual, often housed in a "Special Collections."

Physical Control — The management of archives through their tangible organization resulting from "processing" and taking into account the archival principle of the five levels of arrangement.

Preservation Copy — A duplicate of a record that is often created in an alternative format to the original to help ensure the long-term retention of the information found within that original record.

Preservation Survey — A formal project that assesses the state of materials within a collection by evaluating the materials' housing environment, the storage materials in which the archives are kept, and the condition of the materials themselves.

Primary Source — Unique, recorded information that was created contemporaneously with the time it illustrates, by a person who participated in the recorded events. Primary sources include, but are not limited to, such items as photographs, diaries, and ledgers. They are distinguished from secondary sources.

Processing — The act of organizing, describing, and preserving archival material in a repository to ensure its safety and to make it available for access.

Provenance —
1. The origin of a collection; documents the life of the collection (e.g., donor, previous owners of the collection).
2. The archival strategy of not intermingling records from different creators or donors. The "creator" is an organization or individual who wrote, accumulated, and/or

maintained and used the records in the conduct of their business or personal life.

Public Records — Local, state, or federal government–created documents that serve a public purpose and are subject to laws related to their maintenance and distribution.

Record Group — A large grouping of materials within a collection (e.g., the records created by a department within a municipality may be considered a record group).

Record Life Cycle — Refers to the original purpose for which a record is created and its subsequent uses. A record is most actively used soon after its creation. With the passage of time, the primary purpose for which a document is created elapses or users need to access the document less frequently. The phases of the record life cycle include: Creation, Use, Maintenance (i.e., storage, retrieval, and protection), Disposition (i.e., transfer to less expensive temporary storage area), Destruction, Transfer (to archives).

Records — Documents in any form containing information created by an organization during the course of the institution's daily activities.

Records Management — The function that controls the creation, maintenance, and disposition of information created by an institution. Records management involves controlling the creation of forms and deciding what types of records need to be generated by departments. The records management function also controls the flow of paper through the creation of an inventory and schedules that detail how long paper should be kept and when it should be moved to alternate storage.

Retention Schedule — In records management, the document followed by records managers to determine the disposition of documents in their care. It outlines the appropriate means and time to transfer, dispose, or move records to an archival facility. Some records are subject to regulation, and the imperative for following retention guidelines is strong. The schedule notes how long items need to be retained and what must be done with them after they have lived out their active lives.

Sanctity of Original Order — The archival strategy of maintaining records from full collections in the order that they were kept by the creator.

Scope and Content — The description of a collection or its parts.

Secondary Sources — Nonoriginal and mass-produced materials such as photocopies and published items, including news clippings, books, and journal articles. These materials are generally separated from archival resources for preservation purposes, to distinguish them from primary resources, and to reduce supply costs. These materials are not generally created contemporaneously with the events they describe as the events occur.

Series — Records, generally with the same provenance, that have a similar theme, result from the same activity, or that have similar formats. Within the five levels of arrangement, the level that falls below the fonds. The series records are generally the most commonly described groups of records within archival finding aids — primarily, the descriptive inventory.

Special Collections — Groups of personal papers, such as those generally found in an historical society, usually relating to an individual or family.

Vital Records — Those records essential to the continued functioning of an organization or of prime importance to an individual's life. Vital records include such materials as birth, death, and marriage records; incorporation papers; charters; and deeds.

# Bibliography

Abraham, Terry. *Documentation Strategies: A Decade (or More) Later.* A paper presented at the annual meeting of the Society of American Archivists, Washington, D.C., August 31, 1995. http://www.uidaho.edu/special-collections/papers/docstr10.htm.

Alexander, Phillip N., and Helen W. Samuels. "The Roots of 128: A Hypothetical Documentation Strategy." *The American Archivist* 50 (Fall 1987): 518–531.

An, Xiaomi. "An Integrated Approach to Records Management." *The Information Management Journal* (July/August 2003): 24–30.

Archibald, Robert. *A Place to Remember: Using History to Build Community.* CA: AltaMira Press, 1999.

Arizona Board of Regents on behalf of ASU Lodestar Center for Philanthropy and Nonprofit Innovation. *Models of Collaboration: Nonprofit Organizations Working Together*, 2009. http://www.asu.edu/copp/nonprofit/conf/coll_models_report_FINALDRAFT.pdf.

Backman, Prudence. *Appraisal of Local Government Records for Historical Value.* Albany: The University of the State of New York, 1996

Bearman, David. *Archival Methods.* Pittsburgh: Archives & Museum Informatics, 1989.

. "Archival Strategies" *The American Archivist* 58 (1994): 374–407.

Beasley, Gerald. "Curatorial Crossover: Building Library, Archives and Museums Collections." *RBM: A Journal of Rare Books and Manuscripts* 8.1 (Spring 2007): 20–28.

Bell, Carmine. "Public Education and Community Development: The Shared Mission of Libraries and Cultural Heritage Institutions." Report. http://eric.ed.gov/ERICDocs/data/ericdocs2sql/content_storage_01/0000019b/80/1a/b9/bb.pdf.

Bell, Chauncey. *Organizational Change and the Role of the Archivist.* Keynote Speech at California Society of Archivists meeting. Pasadena California: 1998. Available at http://www.mybestdocs.com/.

. *Organizational Change: What Is It and What Does It Mean for Records Professionals?* Keynote address to National Association of Government Archives and Record Administrators. Sacramento, California, 1997. http://www.mybestdocs.com/.

Benedict, Karen. "Invitation to a Bonfire: Reappraisal and Deaccessioning of Records as Collection Management Tools in an Archives — A Reply to Leonard Rapport." *The American Archivist* 47.1 (Winter 1984): 43–49.

Bishoff, Liz. "The Collaboration Imperative." *Library Journal* 129.1 (January 2004): 34–35.

Blewett, Joan, Joel Genuth, and Spencer R. Weart. *Documenting Multi-Institutional Collaborations*. American Institute of Physics, 2001. Available at http://www.aip.org/history/pubs/collabs/mainreport.pdf.

Blouin, Francis X. "Archivists, Mediation, and the Constructs of Social Memory." *Archival Issues* 24. 2 (1999).

Booms, Hans. "Society and the Formation of a Documentary Heritage: Issues in the Appraisal of Archival Sources." *Archivaria* 24 (Summer 1987): 69–107.

Ed. James Gregory Bradsher. *Managing Archives and Archival Institutions*. Chicago: University of Chicago Press, 1988.

Brophy, Sarah. *Is Your Museum Grant Ready: Assessing Your Organization's Potential for Funding*. MD: AltaMira Press, 2005.

Burgett, James, John Haar, and Linda L. Phillips. *Collaborative Collection Development: A Practical Guide for Your Library.* Chicago: American Library Association, 2004.

Carr, David. *The Promise of Cultural Institutions.* Walnut Creek, CA: AltaMira Press, 2003.

Clareson, Tom. "Collaboration: A Key to Cultural Funding." *Texas Library Journal* 77.128 (Spring 2001): 32–33.

Conwill, Kinshasha Holman and Alexandra Marmion Roosa. "Cultivating Community Connections." *Museum News* (May/June 2003).

Cook, Terry. *The Archival Appraisal of Records Containing Personal Information: A RAMP Study with Guidelines*. Paris: United Nations Educational, Scientific and Cultural Organization, 1991.

. "Archival Science and Postmodernism: New Formulations for Old Concepts." *Archival Science* 1.1 (2000): 3–24. http://www.mybestdocs.com/cook-t-postmod-p1-00.htm.

. "Overview of Appraisal: Why Are We Here This Week." Presentation to Appraisal Seminar. Monash University, Melbourne, VIC Canada. March 15, 1999. Text available at http://www.recordkeeping.com.au/march99/terrycookoverview.html.

. "What Is Past Is Prologue: A History of Archival Ideas Since 1898, and the Future Paradigm Shift." *Archivaria* 43 (Spring 97). http://www.mybestdocs.com/cookt-pastprologue-ar43fnl.htm.

Cox, Richard. *Documenting Localities: A Practical Model for American Archivists and Manuscript Curators.* Chicago: Society of American Archivists, 1996.

Cunningham, Adrian. "Collecting Archives in the Next Millennium," paper presented to the Australian Society of Archivists, July 1997.

Davies, D.W. *Public Libraries as Culture and Social Centers: The Origin of the Concept*. Metuchen, NJ: The Scarecrow Press, Inc., 1974.

Davis, MJ. "Just Say No! Nicely," Bay State Historical League, *Common Wealth* (Winter 1996–97): 2.

Dearstyne, Bruce. *Managing Historical Record Programs: A Guide for Historical Agencies.* Walnut Creek, CA: AltaMira Press, 2000.

Denise, Leo. "Collaboration Vs. C-three (Cooperation, Coordination, and Communication)." *Innovating*. The Rensselaerville Institute. 7.3. N.D. http://www.ride.ri.gov/adulteducation/Documents/Tri%20part%201/Collaboration%20vs.%20the%203c%27s.pdf.

Diamont-Cohen, Betsy, and Dina Sherman. "Hand in Hand: Museums and Libraries Working Together." *Public Libraries* 42.2 (March–April 2003): 102–105.

Doylan, Michael. "Experiments in Deaccessioning: Archives and Online Auctions." *The American Archivist* 64.2 (Fall–Winter 2001): 350–362.

Edwards, Phillip N. "Collection Development and Maintenance Across Libraries, Archives and Museums: A Novel Collaborative Approach." *Library Resources & Technical Services* 48.1 (2004): 26–33.

The Evergreen State Society. "What Should Our Mission Statement Say?" Seattle, Washington: Internet Nonprofit Center, 2003. http://www.nonprofits.org/npofaq/03/21.html.

Fleckner, John A. *Archives and Manuscript Surveys.* Chicago: Society of American Archivists, 1977.

Flinn, Andrew. "'An attack on professionalism and scholarship'?: Democratizing Archives and the Production of Knowledge." *Ariadne* 62 (January 2010). http://wwwariadne.ac.uk/issue62/flinn.

Foster, Ann L. "Montana's Traveling Archivist Project." *Annotation* NHPRC newsletter 29 (March 2001): 6–7. http://www.archives.gov/nhprc/annotation/pdf/2001-mar.pdf.

Furchgott, Richard. "Taxes: What's Your Donation Really Worth? How to Get the Right Appraisal — And the Best Deduction." *Business Week Online* (April 10, 2000). http://www.businessweek.com/2000/00_15/b3676159.htm.

Gates, Christopher T. "Forum: Democracy and the Civic Museum." *Museum News (*May/June 2001). http://www.aam-us.org/pubs/mn/MN_MJ01_DemocracyMuseum.cfm.

Gardner, James B., and Elizabeth E. Merritt, ed. *The AAM Guide to Collections Planning.* Washington, D.C.: American Association of Museums, 2004: 1.

Gehrlich, James L. "The Archival Imagination of David Bearman, Revisited." *Journal of Archival Organization* 1.1 (2002): 5–18.

Gibson, Hannah, Anne Morris, and Marigold Cleeve. "Links Between Libraries and Museums: Investigating Museum-Library Collaboration in England and the USA." *Libri* 57 (2007): 53–64.

Gorman, Michael. "The Wrong Path and the Right Path: The Role of Libraries in Access to and Preservation of Cultural Heritage." *Progressive Librarian* 28 (Winter 2006/2007): 87–100.

Green, Mark A. "I've Deaccessioned and Lived to Tell about It: Confessions of an Unrepentant Reappraiser." *Archival Issues* 30 (2006): 7–22.

. "The Power of Archives: Archivists' Values and Value in the Postmodern Age." *The American Archivist* 72 (Spring/Summer 2009).

. "The Existential Archivist: Use as a Measure of 'Better' Appraisal." Unpublished paper for the Society of

American Archivists Meeting, 1999. http://ahc.uwyo.edu/documents/faculty/greene/papers/SAA%2099%20three.pdf.

. "The Power of Meaning: The Archival Mission in the Postmodern Age." *The American Archivist* 65 (Spring/Summer 2002): 42–55.

Hackman, Larry J., and Joan Warnow-Blewett. "The Documentation Strategy Process: A Model and a Case Study." *The American Archivist* 50 (Winter 1987): 12–47.

. "The Origins of Documentation Strategies in Context: Recollections and Reflections." *The American Archivist* 72 (Fall/Winter 2009): 436–459.

Ham, F. Gerald. "Archival Choices: Managing the Historical Record in an Age of Abundance." *The American Archivist* 47 (Winter 1984): 11–22.

. "The Archival Edge." *The American Archivist* 38 (Jan. 1975): 5–13.

Hedstrom, M., and John Leslie King. "Epistemic Infrastructure in the Rise of the Knowledge Economy." *Advancing Knowledge and the Knowledge Economy*. Edited by Brian Kahin and Dominque Foray. Cambridge, MA: MIT Press, 2007: 113–34.

Hershey Community Archives Collection, Hershey, PA.

Holbrook Gerzina, Gretchen. *Mr. and Mrs. Prince: How an Extraordinary Eighteenth-Century Family Moved Out of Slavery and Into Legend.* New York, NY: Amistad Press, 2008.

Jimerson, Randall C. *Archives Power: Memory, Accountability, and Social Justice*. Chicago: Society of American Archivists, 2009.

Johnson, Elizabeth Snowden. "Our Archives, Our Selves: Documentation Strategy and the Re-Appraisal of Professional Identity." *The American Archivist* 71 (Spring/Summer 2008): 190–202.

Kammen, Carol. *On Doing Local History.* Lanham, MD: AltaMira Press, 2003.

Keggan, P. Burke. *Fundraising for Nonprofits*. New York, NY: HarperCollins Publishers, 1990.

Ketelaar, Eric. *The Archive as a Time Machine.* Closing Speech of the DLM-Forum 2002. Barcelona, 2002. http://www.mybestdocs.com/.

Kreps, Christina F. *Liberating Culture: Cross-Cultural Perspectives on Museums, Curation and Heritage Preservation*. London: Routledge, 2003.

Malaro, Marie C. "Collections Management Policies." *Museum News* (November/December 1979): 57–61.

Malkmus, Doris J. "Documentation Strategy: Mastodon or Retro-Success." *The American Archivist* 71 (Fall/Winter 2008): 384–409.

Mandell, Myrna P. "Types of Collaborations and Why the Differences Really Matter." *The Public Manager* (Winter 2002/2003): 36–40.

Marshall, Jennifer. "Documentation Strategy in the Twenty-First Century? Rethinking Institutional Priorities and Professional Limitations." *Archival Issues* 23.1 (1998): 59–74.

McBee, Shar. *To Lead Is to Serve: How to Attract Volunteers and Keep Them.* 1994. http://www.sharmcbee.com.

McKemmish, Sue. "Yesterday, Today and Tomorrow: A Continuum of Responsibility." *Proceedings of the Records Management Association of Australia 14th National Convention,* 15–17 (Sep. 1997), RMAA Perth.

Parker, Kristin. "The Blurred Line: A Museum Registrar Turns Archivist." *NEA Newsletter* 36.1 (January 2009): 4–6.

Pederson, Ann, ed. "Documentation Programmes for Archives." Chapter 10 in *Keeping Archives*. Sydney, Australia: Australia Society of Archivists Incorporated, 1987.

Phillips, Faye. "Developing Collection Development Policies for Manuscript Collections." *The American Archivist* 47 (Winter 1984): 30–43.

Porter, Daniel R. III. *Current Thoughts on Collections Policy: Producing the Essential Document for Administering Your Collection.* Technical Report 1. American Association for State and Local History.

Raab, Christopher M., and Eric J. Roth. "Documenting New Paltz History: A Case Study in Library — Museum Cooperation." http://dspace.nitle.org/bitstream/handle/10090/2937/NPArticleFinal.pdf?sequence=1.

Rapport, Leonard. "No Grandfather Clause: Reappraising Accessioned Records." *The American Archivist* 44 (Spring 1981): 143–50.

Reed-Scott, Jutta. "Collection Management Strategies for Archivists." *The American Archivist* 47 (Winter 1984): 24–29.

Ridener, John. *From Polders to Postmodernism: A Concise History of Archival Theory*. Duluth, Minnesota: Litwin Books LLC, 2008.

Samuels, Helen Willa. "Who Controls the Past." *The American Archivist* 49 (Spring 1986): 109–123.

"Improving Our Disposition: Documentation Strategy." *Archivaria* 33 (Winter 1991–92)

. *Varsity Letters: Documenting Modern Colleges and Universities.* Chicago: Society of American Archivists, 1992.

Sanford, Gregory, and Ann Lawless. "Regrants and Collaboration: A View from Vermont's Northeast Kingdom." *Annotation* NHPRC newsletter 29 (March 2001): 1, 10.

Sauer, Cynthia K. "Doing the Best We Can? The Use of Collection Development Policies and Cooperative Collecting Activities at Manuscript Repositories." *The American Archivist* 64 (Fall/Winter 2001): 308–349.

Schellenberg, Theodore. "The Appraisal of Modern Public Records." National Archives Bulletin 8: National Archives and Records Service, 1956. Reprinted in Ed. Maygene, F. Daniels and Timothy Walch. *A Modern Archives Reader: Basic Readings on Archival Theory and Practice*. Washington, D.C.: National Archives and Records Service, 1984.

Schrage, Michael. "The Rules of Collaboration." *Indiana Libraries* 18 suppl. 3–4 (1999): 1.

______. "Collaboration and Creativity." *Museum News* (March/April 2004). http://www.aam-us.org/pubs/mn/MN_MA04_CollabCreativ.cfm.

Seton, Rosemary. *The Preservation and Administration of Private Archives: A RAMP Study*. Paris: General Information Program and UNISIST, 1984. http://unesdoc.unesco.org/images/0005/000596/059687e.pdf.

Taylor, Hugh. "Clio in the Raw: Archival Materials and the Teaching of History." *The American Archivist* (July/October 1972): 317–330.

Waibel, Gunter, and Rick Erway. "Think Global, Act Local: Library, Archives and Museum Collaboration." *Museum Management and Curatorship* 24.4 (2009). http://www.oclc.org/research/publications/library/2009/waibel-erway-mmc.pdf.

Walch, Victoria Irons. *Maintaining State Records in an Era of Change: A National Challenge — A Report on State Archives and Records Management Programs.* Council of State Historical Records Coordinators, 1996.

______. "Recognizing Leadership and Partnership: A Report on the Condition of Historical Records in the States and Efforts to Ensure Their Preservation and Use." Council of State Historical Records Coordinators, 1993.

Weil, Stephen E., ed. *A Deaccession Reader.* Washington, D.C.: American Association of Museums, 1997.

Weinberg, David M. "The Impact of Grantsmaking: An Evaluation of Archival and Records Management Programs at the Local Level." *The American Archivist* Vol. 62 (Fall 1999): 247–70.

White, Grant. "Message in a Bottle: Community Memory in the Local Studies Collection," *Australian Public Libraries and Information Services* 13.3 (September 2000): 96–101.

Wilson, Ian E. "Towards a Vision of Archival Services." *Archivaria* 31 (Winter 1990–91): 91–99.

Wisconsin Historical Records Advisory Board and Wisconsin Association of Public Librarians. *Creating a Collection Development Policy for Local History Records in Public Libraries.* April 1998. http://www.wisconsinhistory.org/libraryarchives/whrab/wapl.pdf.

Yarrow, Alexandra, Barbara Clubb, and Jennifer-Lynn Draper. "Public Libraries, Archives and Museums: Trends in Collaboration and Cooperation." IFLA Professional Reports, No. 108. International Federation of Library Associations and Institutions, 2008.

Zorich, Diane M., Gunter Waibel, and Ricky Erway. *Beyond the Silos of the LAMs: Among Library, Archives and Museums*. Dublin, OH: OCLC, 2008.

# Index

www.ingramcontent.com/pod-product-compliance
Lightning Source LLC
LaVergne TN
LVHW050615100826
845148LV00011B/1601

*9780982727607*